TH_____ue in
the_____
pape_____tains
the works of a single poet, along with an
original introduction, a chronology of the
poet's career, a bibliography and notes
on the poetry.

ANDREWS WANNING has contributed
critical reviews and articles to such
periodicals as "Furioso," "The Southern
Review," "Partisan Review," "Kenyon
Review," and "Focus." A graduate of Yale
University, Professor Wanning studied with
I. A. Richards at the University of
Cambridge where he received his doctorate.
He teaches at Bard College and is engaged
in the writing of a work on seventeenth-
century literature.

RICHARD WILBUR, the General Editor,
has won the Pulitzer Prize, the National
Book Award, and the Millay Prize, all
three in 1957 for his book of poems,
"Things of This World." His most recent
volume of poetry is "Advice to a Prophet."
Professor Wilbur has held a Guggenheim
and a Prix de Rome Fellowship and is a
member of the National Institute of Arts
and Letters. He is now Professor of
English at Wesleyan University.

The Laurel Poetry Series
General Editor, Richard Wilbur

Donne

Selected, with an introduction
and notes, by Andrews Wanning

Published by
DELL PUBLISHING CO., INC.
750 Third Avenue
New York 17, N.Y.

The poems in this edition are taken from THE POEMS
OF JOHN DONNE, edited by Herbert J. C. Grierson
(1912), and THE DIVINE POEMS by John Donne, edited
by Helen Gardner (1952), The Clarendon Press,
Oxford. Reprinted by permission of the publisher.

Typography by Alvin Eisenman

Cover drawing by Richard Powers

First printing: August, 1962
Second printing: December, 1964
Third printing: October, 1965
Fourth printing: October, 1966
Fifth printing: February, 1968

Printed in U.S.A.

Contents

Introduction

No major poet has more than Donne reflected in the gyrations of his reputation the changing taste of the centuries. To his contemporaries he ruled, in Carew's phrase, "the universal monarchy of wit"; even the bad-tempered Ben Jonson, so reluctant to admit eminence beyond his own, allowed that he was "the first poet in the world in some things." Two generations later Dryden still chose Donne to flatter the Earl of Dorset by comparison; but in an age newly conscious of a feminine audience, he reprehended him for "perplexing the minds of the fair sex with nice speculations of philosophy, when he should engage their hearts and entertain them with the softnesses of love." A century still later, Samuel Johnson, caught between a native respect for intelligence and a poetic theory that disavowed the exceptional in favor of the general, demolished Donne (though he spoke more largely of the epigones of his school) with a lingering admiration. "To write on their plan," he said, "it was at least necessary to read and think."

In the hundred years following Johnson the taste for Donne virtually disappeared save for a few inquisitive antiquarian gourmets like Coleridge and De Quincey. In that monument to Victorian taste, *The Golden Treasury of Songs and Lyrics,* Palgrave (whose chief adviser was Tennyson) could find room for only one poem by, so he thought, Donne; it is perhaps *not* surprising that the single poem was a harmless song now generally attributed to John Hoskins. But this was the bottom. In the last quarter of the nineteenth century Gosse's *Life* and the editions of

Grosart, Norton, and Chambers reflected the growing interest of scholars and students; in the early twentieth Grierson's monumental edition in 1912 and his anthology of Metaphysical Poetry in 1921 both reflected and led the growing understanding and explanation of the ways of Donne and his followers. The anthology was the text (and very largely the inspiration) for T. S. Eliot's famous manifesto on the Metaphysicals, in reality concerned no less with the practice of modern poetry than with the comprehension of Donne. For Eliot a chasm yawned in the middle of the seventeenth century; before it Donne and his school "possessed a mechanism which could devour any kind of experience," after it the English poets "thought and felt by fits, unbalanced; they reflected." Modern poetry sought to repossess the devouring mechanism; this writer, who began to read English poetry seriously at the end of the twenties, remembers the heady sympathies of those days. The cause of Donne was the cause of modern poetry; it was heresy only to the mossbacks to equal his name with the greatest in English poetry (Shakespeare only excepted). No doubt we view him now with less partiality and with a less combative enthusiasm. But it is incredible to suppose that he will ever again be regarded as no more than a crotchety minor lyricist.

It is to be observed that in all this Odyssey of taste there is little evidence of any real disagreement as to the special nature of Donne's poetry. Throughout, the key word is "wit," from Carew's eulogy of the universal monarch, to Johnson's definition of wit as "the discovery of occult resemblances in things apparently unlike," to George Williamson's summary of "the rule of wit" as his chief characteristic. The taste for Donne has, in short, fluctuated pretty generally with the taste for wit in poetry, or at least with the taste for wit in the surprising mixtures Donne compounded. Somewhere around 1818 Coleridge produced a critical summary in two couplets which for condensed suggestiveness has not been surpassed:

> With Donne, whose muse on dromedary trots,
> Wreathe iron pokers into true-love knots;

> Rhyme's sturdy cripple, fancy's maze and clue,
> Wit's forge and fire-blast, meaning's press and screw.

The eighteenth century had indeed cultivated wit in poetry, but it had balked at the dromedary trots and the iron pokers. The nineteenth on the whole found wit of a lowering tendency, though it could license it when it masqueraded as frivolity (Hood and Praed) or nonsense (Carroll and Lear). Our own century, intent on apprehending variety and complexity, has been ready indeed to turn to wit—the language of paradox and "impure" poetry—as the creative forge in which to "unify" sensibility and devour any kind of experience.

Our notions of what we would wish to do, or so it seems to me, have somewhat influenced our notions of what Donne did. If in rebellion against Victorian high seriousness, we have also wanted to exonerate wit from frivolity, and in the context of discussion of important purposes, a certain solemnity has sometimes crept in. To look for uniformly important purposes in Donne is often to misread him; and whatever else he was, he was *not* a solemn poet.

"Wit" is of course a word of protean usages, never more so than in the seventeenth century when it might run the gamut from the working of the mind generally—or even the perceptions—to a skill in bawdy jokes. Donne himself uses it—both the word and the wide context of qualities it denotes—in a large variety of ways in his poetry (he is not without the bawdy jokes). Certainly we cannot wholly understand these usages through trying to restore the expectations that "wit" aroused in his contemporary audience. No genuine poet writes only according to the recipes of current rhetorics or current fashion. But the recipes can provide us with a certain dry scale, less subjectively calibrated than modern interpretations, against which we can try to measure his achievements and his departures.

By and large the Elizabethan poet (and Donne's love songs and elegies are almost all Elizabethan in date) was not expected to be a critic of life or an explorer of his own soul; he was expected to be a performer, indeed an entertainer. The graver sort of critic, especially in justifying poetry in the face of the Puritans, followed the lead of Horace's "docere et diligare"; but even Sir Philip Sidney in his *Defense* turned the case more nearly to instructing *through* delighting, and visibly relished the delighting. William Webbe, surveying poets *ab origine*, found frankly that "most of them had speciall regarde to the pleasant-nesse of theyr fine conceytes, whereby they might drawe mens mindes into admiration of theyr inventions, more than they had to the profitte or commoditye that the Readers shoulde reape by their works." However this description applies to the ages, it is suggestive enough of (and was no doubt suggested by) the actual workings of those of his contemporaries who practiced the art of the short love lyric or song. They were not much concerned to improve or explore; a shorter definition of their practice might be borrowed from Sir Thomas Overbury's nutshell summary of the character form: "wit's descant on any plain song."

In fact the plain song for these lyrical descants came from the elaborate conventions of Petrarchan postures whose center was the adoration of the ideally chaste (and therefore cruel) beauty; and alternatively from the possible variety of comment on the convention by any unromantic man—who was sometimes cast in pastoral shape as the simple, and therefore sensible hind. In spite of elaboration, the range of subjects, whether Petrarchan or anti-Petrarchan, was not great; and they became, in effect, standard exercises for the display of talent in variation by the individual virtuoso: wit's descant, or the pleasantness of his fine conceits. The subjects being largely in the public domain, the procedure obviously put high value on execution, and therefore on individual novelty, surprise, ingenuity. The technical term for the faculty for finding out the means of adorning the idea was invention, which George Gascoigne considered "the first and most necessarie poynt in making of a *delectable* poeme." An example he gives may be a fair sample of the state of mind of the courtly poet in confronting composition: "Likewise, if I should disclose my pretence in love [of course a standard subject] I would eyther make a strange discourse of some intollerable passion, or finde occasion to pleade by the example of some historie, or discover my disquiet in shadowes *per Allegoriam,* or use the covertest mean that I could to avoyde the uncomely customes of common writers."

If this sounds to the delicate modern ear like a recipe for the deliberate manufacture of witty poems, it was certainly so intended by Gascoigne. Did Donne share this possibly unromantic attitude toward creation? Did he, in short, write at least at times out of deliberation rather than passion? No doubt the question is too bald for absolute generalization, and at this remove it is hardest of all to be sure about intentions. But we do know that Donne when he began to write was a fashionable young man-about-town engaged in a fashionable activity for young men-about-town: he was, a contemporary wrote, "a great Visiter of Ladies, a great Frequenter of Plays, a great Writer of conceited Verses." And it is certainly a fair internal inference from at least some of his poems that he delighted in entertaining with wit, in startling with ingenuity, and sometimes in shocking with perversity.

Yet Donne did not, as did the army of sonneteers (Shakespeare, and perhaps Spenser, excepted) who responded to the same challenge in the 1590's, merely play ingenious changes on the extant forms of Petrarchan metaphors and hyperboles. Or, to put it in Gascoigne's terms, he did not merely devise "strange discourses" or new "histories" and "shadowes *per Allegoriam.*" He radically altered the forms themselves. It is true that it is possible to argue, as Miss Rosemond Tuve has most impressively done, that for each of his changes technically defined some sort of precedent can be found. But to take this historical analysis of partial techniques for a conclusion (which Miss Tuve did not quite do) is to overlook the profound originality of the whole. Whatever the psychological sources of Donne's endeavors in poetry, the *effect* is of a powerful and in some way consistent personality: extreme, violent, and iconoclastic, not in spite of, but because of its wit.

Regarded technically, Donne altered the forms of his

given tradition in three main ways. Regarded more subjectively, the technical changes, it is important to note,
had each the effect of further dramatizing the personality.
First of all, he colloquialized the language: he used the
wiry and often harsh rhythms of the spoken voice, as well
as its informal, and often elliptical, syntax. He used, too,
a vocabulary that has the ring of talk; but the effect of it
was not to narrow but to broaden the traditional range of
poetic idiom. Notably he did *not* confine himself to the
simplified and purified vocabulary of the traditional pastoral swain; he used his own natural idiom, the multi-
faceted vocabulary of an inquisitive man educated to both
town and gown.

Donne's openings in this style have long been celebrated:

> For Godsake hold your tongue, and let me love . . .

> I wonder by my troth, what thou, and I
> Did, till we lov'd. . . .

> I am two fooles, I know,
> For loving, and for saying so
> In whining Poëtry. . . .

> Who ever loves, if he do not propose
> The right true end of love, he's one that goes
> To sea for nothing but to make him sick. . . .

But the continuations and endings are as arresting, though
since by the logic of Donne's peculiar structure they have
the preceding weight of the poem behind them, it is less
satisfying to quote them in isolation:

> Love's not so pure, and abstract, as they use
> To say, which have no Mistresse but their Muse. . . .

> He ruin'd mee, and I am re-begot
> Of absence, darknesse, death; things which are
>   not. . . .

> My ragges of heart can like, wish, and adore,
> But after one such love, can love no more.

> Nor praise, nor dispraise me, nor blesse nor curse
> Openly loves force, nor in Bed fright thy Nurse
> With midnights starting, crying out, oh, oh
> Nurse, ô my love is slaine, I saw him goe
> O'r the white Alpes alone; I saw him I,
> Assail'd, fight, taken, stabb'd, bleed, fall, and die.

These may be, in the language of Gascoigne, "strange discourses of some intolerable passions." But the effect is far more than a technical alteration of diction: what it does is to bring to life the speaking voice of the poet, vivid and impromptu. It dramatizes the character; indeed it is far closer to the diction of contemporary playwrights than of lyric poets (one of the few persuasive precedents in nondramatic poetry is the work of a playwright, Marlowe in his rough translation of Ovid's *Elegies,* from which Donne may well have borrowed his own title). As with other dramatic characters, the voice may be a mask; if so, the illusion is none the less compelling.

Donne's second major technical innovation was to make the intellectual framework of the poem an essential part of its poetic texture. For the lyrical, basically reiterative form of the typical Elizabethan lyric he substituted a tough, involved, often paradoxical and frequently elusive reasoning that moves throughout the poem. The reader knows this instinctively simply by his awareness of the logical demands the poems make on him for constant pursuit of the argument. Technically the difference may perhaps be most graphically illustrated by a comparison of the role of the stanza in the structural form; for convenient example let us take Marlowe's celebrated "Come Live with Me and Be My Love" and Donne's parody of it, "The Baite." Marlowe's charming poem is a variation-on-the-theme: the stanzas successively detail "all the pleasures" which the opening promises. But the stanzas in "The Baite" are merely stages in a continuing development; though a *jeu d'esprit* the poem builds logically to justify its whimsical conclusion:

> That fish, that is not catch'd thereby,
> Alas, is wiser farre then I.

The variation-on-the-theme, or some such simple logical echo as the proposition-and-response form of the octave and sestet of the sonnet, is the characteristic overall structure of the pre-Donne lyric. But in almost all of Donne's the argument moves, progresses, twists, probes, analyzes —frequently in quite fantastic ways.

Again the dramatizing effect is considerable: it is this turbulent logic that lies behind what Grierson called "the peculiar blend of passion and thought, feeling and ratiocination which is their [the lyrics'] greatest achievement," and which Eliot paraphrased, in a celebrated phrase, as "a direct sensuous apprehension of thought, or a re-creation of thought into feeling." Eliot's phrase, linked as it was with his theory as to a later dissociation of thought and feeling, has been a main stamping-ground for modern critical study of Donne and his descendants, though it cannot be said that in the course of it the exact workings of the indicated alchemy have grown much clearer. The word "sensuous" is confusing: Donne is not a poet (like Spenser) who especially excites the senses, the special perceptions of eye, ear, touch, and so forth. I should say rather that the very great excitement of the poems is conveyed through ideas (as rarely with Spenser); or more precisely that we are so caught up in the rush of thought, the poise, pounce, and reckless dart of ideas made manifest, that we are made to feel so much restless energy of mind must be the effect of passion rather than of cool device.

This passionate logic works in collaboration with the third of Donne's chief technical developments: what has long been discussed as the metaphysical conceit, what Henry Wells has called the radical image, what Johnson long ago pointed to somewhat disapprovingly as "*discordia concors*, the discovery of occult resemblances in things apparently unlike, the most heterogeneous ideas yoked by violence together." Actually the strangeness of association itself, even the elaborate working out of the details are the least original of Donne's major achievements. The Elizabethans loved extravagant tropes, ingenious and covert conceits and allegories; Donne is different here chiefly in degree and in violence of extremity. What is more essentially different is their function: the Elizabethan poem generally proceeds by what I call the Metaphor of Foregone Conclusion, Donne by the Metaphor of Unknown Conclusion. That is to say in the characteristic Elizabethan poem the relationship has already been stated, the conceit falls comfortably into place as illustration, in that sense is decorative. With Donne the image explodes without warning, weaves, amplifies, surprises; the vibrations of meaning are established through its workings alone, and not infrequently—as in, for example, "A Feaver," "A Valediction: of weeping," or "A Lecture upon the Shadow"—it *is* the poem. Nothing gives more immediately the sense of discovery in action which is so much a part of the movement of a Donne lyric.

But we must also recognize that the means that produce these important effects are also precisely what the age recognized as the sources of Donne's extraordinary wit, including the more deliberate and manufactured kind. Especially the last two: paradoxical and fantastic argument and ingenious discovery of elaborate metaphorical parallels are the very heart and center of the exercise of Invention, the soul of Wit. It is true that the age recognized something more than conventional in Donne's: Carew's terms are "imperious wit" and "Giant Phansie." It is true, on the other hand, that many of Donne's poems *are* fun, *jeux d'esprit*, gambits for bravado—and not only the Epigrams. Yet even the lightest poems have usually the singeing of some serious inquiry. "The Flea," for example, which by its first position in the 1635–1669 editions suggests seventeenth-century taste, is a free-wheeling jest on the ever-popular theme of Persuasions (or seductions) to Love. But it carries a weight which its Restoration counterparts lack because its blasphemy is genuine. It shudders at the sanctities it mocks: honor, the marriage contract, the sacraments, more particularly at the possibility that its parody of "our marriage bed, and marriage temple" may be no more than true. Contrariwise, there are few poems of Donne so solemn as not to contain also some sacrilegious levity. "The Extasie," though a most subtle and philosophical investigation of the relations of soul and body, is perfectly aware of the absurdity of the posture of the lover and the outsized ammunition it uses in the cause of another Persuasion to Love. The "Hymne to God my God, in my sicknesse," conceived in the expectation of death, makes fun of the "flat map" to which he is reduced and plays with the gaiety of enjoyment on the paradoxes of Christian faith. Whether the tone be chiefly gay or chiefly sober, the methods of wit, the extreme pursuit of logic or metaphor, are also in the service of discovery in a less technical sense: the discovery of a variety of attitudes, often of paradoxical attitudes toward a human situation. Though it is again well to remember that the discovery can be of what Miss Tuve calls general truth rather than of the poet's private experience.

The subject matter for general truth is often provided by a perfectly traditional point of departure; as a result another source of the shock of wit in the poetry is the contention between conventional matter and the original and peculiar in Donne's treatment. Students of his religious thinking have invariably found it orthodoxly Catholic both in theology and in the devotional forms he uses; indeed it seems likely that he was able to make the transition from the Roman to the Anglican faiths because orthodox Anglicanism presented no severe innovations to the theology in which he was trained. Yet orthodox Anglicans, like T. S. Eliot and Douglas Bush, have often been made uncomfortable by what is incorrigibly personal in his religious poetry, that same extreme, violent, and even iconoclastic personality. "A Litanie" is based on the traditional, impersonal form of the Prayer Book; it is nevertheless a highly personal poem, in its quirks and in its peculiar awareness of the vanities in virtue:

> When wee are mov'd to seeme religious
> Only to vent wit, Lord deliver us.

Helen Gardner and Louis Martz have pointed out how deeply the *Holy Sonnets* are based on the traditional devotional forms of the meditation; yet the emotion in them is unmistakably Donne's, the posture of the devotee before

God not wholly unreminiscent of the younger Donne's before his mistress. Those two great, craggy, and strangely beautiful poems, *The Anniversaries*, combine, to us as well as to Ben Jonson somewhat incompatibly, two contemporary conventions: the secular form of extravagant eulogy, and the devotional form of meditations on the Contempt of the World and the Glories of Paradise. Yet the mood and texture are incontestably made out of Donne's peculiar imagination and temperament; and the deeply traditional themes are made to accommodate a critique of the world in terms of his awareness of what was new and radically upsetting in research and speculative philosophy.

It may have been less often observed that in the *Songs and Sonets* the peculiar shock of Donne often comes from his taking quite literally and seriously—for purposes of examination—some perfectly conventional theme or idea. In a slight poem like "The Legacie" the wry, deprecatory humor emerges from a detailed visualization of the Valentine notion of lovers exchanging hearts. In a graver poem like "A Valediction: forbidding mourning," the images give literal, and therefore emotional validity to the vague idea of spiritual bonds between lovers. In "Twicknam garden" Donne pursues with ferocity the old Petrarchan irony of the incompatibility between the lover's despair and the burgeoning garden (compare Lodge's "The earth, late choked with showers") and discovers in it a savage mockery of himself, and of love. And continually—in, for example, "The good-morrow," "The Sunne Rising," "A Feaver," "The Anniversarie," "Aire and Angels," "The Canonization," "The Valedictions: of weeping," and "of the booke"—he explores the basic Elizabethan image of the microcosm, of the little world of man epitomizing the great world, and proves through it not a metaphor but some version of his own peculiar truth.

This may be some paradigm of Donne's special accomplishment. His ideas, taken as nutshell paraphrases, are not new. The experience behind the poems may be the imagination's general truths, not personal biography. The techniques may have their partial precedents, and even in their innovations may have responded to the contemporary demands of Witty Invention. But the techniques are shaped by, and record, a consistent and powerful personality, restless and inquisitive. The poems are explorations by that personality. No old truth is taken on faith, and because that is so, each has the impact of one known intimately in its variety of meaning. No convention emerges unchanged. Wit is the "forge and fire-blast" in which Donne converts the materials his age gave him to the shock of discovery every new reader can test for himself.

A word about the selection and text. It has been found possible to include all the *Songs and Sonets* unquestionably Donne's; virtually all of the *Divine Poems* except "The Lamentations of Jeremy," which I think no one will lament; the two long *Anniversaries;* plus substantial selections from the *Elegies, Satyres,* verse letters, *Epithalamions,* and *Epigrams.* All poems are printed complete. The specialist will of course want the unabridged poems, but I think the common reader may feel assured that he is not missing any essential aspect of Donne's genius.

The text, by kind permission of the Oxford University Press, is that of Helen Gardner for *The Divine Poems,* of Grierson as revised for the Oxford Standard Authors in 1933 for all the rest. They are in my opinion the best available. But since all Donne texts are somewhat eclectic, he having authorized none in his own lifetime, I have ventured to alter in a few places Grierson's choice of readings. Where the changes at all affect the meaning, I have given my reasons in the notes. In a very few cases I have silently chosen an alternate spelling in the interest of clarity to the modern reader. But the old spelling and punctuation have been retained, not out of antiquarianism, but because any modernization seems to me to soften Donne's peculiar sound, angularity, and emphasis.

Donne being a special case, the notes at the end are somewhat more elaborate than for most of this series. Without attempting to explain the poems, they make some effort to repair the effects of the lapse of time on general knowledge, and occasionally to suggest certain unfamiliar matters for consideration. I should add that I have occasionally borrowed from the Oxford editors' learning without specific acknowledgment.

ANDREWS WANNING
April, 1962

BIBLIOGRAPHY

Except for Helen Gardner's edition of *The Divine Poems* (Oxford, 1952), Sir Herbert Grierson's path-finding work on *The Poems* is still the basic text (Oxford, 2 vols., 1912). A slightly revised text is also available in a single volume in the Oxford Standard Authors (1933), but without the valuable appendices and notes. Editions by Miss Gardner of other sections of the text are in process, and as they appear will doubtless supersede Grierson as scholarly authority. The most convenient edition of the complete poetry along with large samples of the prose is the Modern Library's (1952), edited by Charles M. Coffin, and based on John Hayward's text, which differs only slightly from Grierson's.

The primary source for Donne's life is Izaak Walton's contemporary *Life of Dr. Donne* (1640, enlarged 1658 and 1675), which is also immensely readable. Edmund Gosse's *The Life and Letters of John Donne* (2 vols., 1899), though erratic and somewhat sentimental, contains much basic material. The most recent critical biography is J. B. Leishman's *The Monarch of Wit* (London, 1951).

The most celebrated early criticism of Donne and the Metaphysical Poets is to be found in Johnson's *Life of Cowley;* any serious student of Donne should read it. The path-finding studies in modern critical re-appraisal of Donne and his successors are Grierson's Introduction to his *Metaphysical Lyrics and Poems* (Oxford, 1921) and T. S.

Eliot's "The Metaphysical Poets" (in his *Selected Essays*, New York, 1950), written as a review of Grierson. Here follows a very partial list of succeeding critical and scholarly studies which the student should find useful:

Alvarez, A., *The School of Donne* (New York, 1961).

Bennett, Joan, *Four Metaphysical Poets* (Cambridge, 1934).

Brooks, Cleanth, *Modern Poetry and the Tradition* (Chapel Hill, 1939); *The Well Wrought Urn* (New York, 1947).

Bush, Douglas, *English Literature in the Earlier Seventeenth Century* (Oxford, 1945). A conservative survey of the religious poetry and prose.

Coffin, C. M., *John Donne and the New Philosophy* (New York, 1937). A study of Donne's use of his intellectual background.

Leavis, F. R., "The Line of Wit," in *Revaluation* (New York, 1947).

Martz, L. L., *The Poetry of Meditation* (New Haven, 1954). Donne's use of traditional devotional forms.

Nicolson, Marjorie, *The Breaking of the Circle* (Evanston, 1950). A study of *The Anniversaries* and their significance in intellectual history.

Praz, Mario, "Donne's Relation to the Poetry of His Time," in *The Flaming Heart* (Anchor Books, New York, 1958).

Spencer, Theodore (ed.), *A Garland for John Donne* (Cambridge, Mass., 1931). Essays by T. S. Eliot, Evelyn Simpson, Mario Praz, John Hayward, M. P. Ramsay, John Sparrow, George Williamson, and Theodore Spencer.

Sypher, Wylie, "Mannerism," in *Four Stages of Renaissance Style* (Anchor Books, New York, 1955). Speculative analogies between expressive style in Donne and in contemporary Mannerist art.

Tuve, Rosemond, *Elizabethan and Metaphysical Imagery* (Chicago, 1947). The poetic and rhetorical traditions behind Metaphysical Poetry. Debated by William Empson, "Donne and the Rhetorical Tradition," *Kenyon Review*, XI, 4, 1949.

Unger, Leonard, *Donne's Poetry and Modern Criticism* (Chicago, 1950).

White, Helen, *The Metaphysical Poets* (New York, 1936). Chiefly the religious poetry.

Williamson, George, *The Donne Tradition* (Cambridge, Mass., 1930; Noonday Paperbound, 1958).

Chronology

1572 Born in London, his father a prosperous London merchant, his mother the descendant of notable Catholic families.

1584–1587 At Hart Hall, Oxford University.

1587 Transferred to Trinity College, Cambridge. No record of a degree at either university, presumably because of religious disability.

1592–1594 Studied law at Lincoln's Inn, London.

1596, 1597 With Essex's expeditions against Cadiz and the Azores.

Before 1600 Period of most of the love poems, elegies, and satires. "A great Visiter of Ladies, a great Frequenter of Plays, a great Writer of conceited Verses."

1598–1602 Secretary to Sir Thomas Egerton, the Lord Keeper.

1601 Secret marriage to Anne More, Egerton's niece.

1602 Dismissed and imprisoned after discovery of marriage. "John Donne—Anne Donne—Undone."

1602–1604 Residence with Sir Francis Wooley at Pyrford.

1605–1609 Residence at Mitcham.

1605–1607 Assisted Thomas Morton (later Bishop of Chester, Lichfield, and Durham) in polemical writing *against* Catholics.

1607 Likely beginning of composition of divine poems ("La Corona").

1608 Composition of *Biathanatos* (a qualified apology for suicide).

1609 Probable date of at least first six of *Holy Sonnets*.

1610–1612 Residence and continental travel with Sir Robert Drury.

1611, 1612 Composition and publication of the two *Anniversaries*, in commemoration of Drury's daughter Elizabeth, died 1610 at 15.

1615 Ordained priest January; Doctor of Divinity, Cambridge, April. Presented to the livings of Keyston and Sevenoaks.

1616–1622 Reader in Divinity at Lincoln's Inn.

1617 Death of his wife (after having borne twelve children and lost five).

1619–1620 With Lord Doncaster's embassy to Germany.

1621 Appointed Dean of Saint Paul's.

1623 Serious illness leading to composition of *Devotions* (pub. 1624).

1624 Appointed Vicar of St. Dunstan's in the West.

1625 Residence at Chelsea with Lady Magdalene Danvers, mother of George Herbert, during plague in London.

1631 Final illness. *Death's Duel* preached Feb. 12, "the Doctor's Own Funeral Sermon." Died March 21.

1633 First collected edition of poems. Seven published by 1669.

1640 Publication of *LXXX Sermons*, with Walton's *Life*.

The good-morrow

I wonder by my troth, what thou, and I*
Did, till we lov'd? were we not wean'd till then?
But suck'd on countrey pleasures, childishly?
Or snorted we in the seaven sleepers den?
T'was so; But this, all pleasures fancies bee.
If ever any beauty I did see,
Which I desir'd, and got, t'was but a dreame of thee.

And now good morrow to our waking soules,
Which watch not one another out of feare;
For love, all love of other sights controules,   10
And makes one little roome, an every where.
Let sea-discoverers to new worlds have gone,
Let Maps to other, worlds on worlds have showne,
Let us possesse one world, each hath one, and is one.

My face in thine eye, thine in mine appeares,
And true plain hearts doe in the faces rest,
Where can we finde two better hemispheares
Without sharpe North, without declining West?
What ever dyes, was not mixt equally;
If our two loves be one, or, thou and I   20
Love so alike, that none doe slacken, none can die.

Song

Goe, and catche a falling starre,
    Get with child a mandrake roote,
Tell me, where all past yeares are,
    Or who cleft the Divels foot,
Teach me to heare Mermaides singing,
    Or to keep off envies stinging,

* Notes appear together, beginning on page 176.

                    And finde
                    What winde
Serves to advance an honest minde.

If thou beest borne to strange sights,   10
    Things invisible to see,
Ride ten thousand daies and nights,
    Till age snow white haires on thee,
Thou, when thou retorn'st, wilt tell mee
All strange wonders that befell thee,
                    And sweare
                    No where
Lives a woman true, and faire.

If thou findst one, let mee know,
    Such a Pilgrimage were sweet;   20
Yet doe not, I would not goe,
    Though at next doore wee might meet,
Though shee were true, when you met her,
And last, till you write your letter,
                    Yet shee
                    Will bee
False, ere I come, to two, or three.

Womans constancy

Now thou hast lov'd me one whole day,
To morrow when thou leav'st, what wilt thou say?
Wilt thou then Antedate some new made vow?
                    Or say that now
We are not just those persons, which we were?
Or, that oathes made in reverentiall feare
Of Love, and his wrath, any may forsweare?
Or, as true deaths, true maryages untie,
So lovers contracts, images of those,
Binde but till sleep, deaths image, them unloose?   10
            Or, your owne end to Justifie,
For having purpos'd change, and falsehood; you
Can have no way but falsehood to be true?

Vaine lunatique, against these scapes I could
              Dispute, and conquer, if I would,
              Which I abstaine to doe,
For by to morrow, I may thinke so too.

The undertaking

I have done one braver thing
    Then all the *Worthies* did,
And yet a braver thence doth spring,
    Which is, to keepe that hid.

It were but madnes now t'impart
    The skill of specular stone,
When he which can have learn'd the art
    To cut it, can finde none.

So, if I now should utter this,
    Others (because no more   10
Such stuffe to worke upon, there is,)
    Would love but as before.

But he who lovelinesse within
    Hath found, all outward loathes,
For he who colour loves, and skinne,
    Loves but their oldest clothes.

If, as I have, you also doe
    Vertue'attir'd in woman see,
And dare love that, and say so too,
    And forget the Hee and Shee;   20

And if this love, though placed so,
    From prophane men you hide,
Which will no faith on this bestow,
    Or, if they doe, deride:

Then you have done a braver thing

Then all the *Worthies* did;
And a braver thence will spring,
   Which is, to keepe that hid.

The Sunne Rising

   Busie old foole, unruly Sunne,
      Why dost thou thus,
Through windowes, and through curtaines call on us?
Must to thy motions lovers seasons run?
      Sawcy pedantique wretch, goe chide
      Late schoole boyes, and sowre prentices,
   Goe tell Court-huntsmen, that the King will ride,
   Call countrey ants to harvest offices;
Love, all alike, no season knowes, nor clyme,
Nor houres, dayes, moneths, which are the rags of time.

   Thy beames, so reverend, and strong   11
      Why shouldst thou thinke?
I could eclipse and cloud them with a winke,
But that I would not lose her sight so long:
      If her eyes have not blinded thine,
      Looke, and to morrow late, tell mee,
   Whether both the'India's of spice and Myne
   Be where thou leftst them, or lie here with mee.
Aske for those Kings whom thou saw'st yesterday,
And thou shalt heare, All here in one bed lay.   20

   She'is all States, and all Princes, I,
      Nothing else is.
Princes doe but play us; compar'd to this,
All honor's mimique; All wealth alchimie.
      Thou sunne art halfe as happy'as wee,
      In that the world's contracted thus;
   Thine age askes ease, and since thy duties bee
   To warme the world, that's done in warming us.
Shine here to us, and thou art every where;
This bed thy center is, these walls, thy sphaere.   30

The Indifferent

I can love both faire and browne,
Her whom abundance melts, and her whom want betraies,
Her who loves lonenesse best, and her who maskes and
    plaies,
Her whom the country form'd, and whom the town,
Her who beleeves, and her who tries,
Her who still weepes with spungie eyes,
And her who is dry corke, and never cries;
I can love her, and her, and you and you,
I can love any, so she be not true.

Will no other vice content you?   10
Will it not serve your turn to do, as did your mothers?
Or have you all old vices spent, and now would finde out
    others?
Or doth a feare, that men are true, torment you?
Oh we are not, be not you so,
Let mee, and doe you, twenty know.
Rob mee, but binde me not, and let me goe.
Must I, who came to travaile thorow you,
Grow your fixt subject, because you are true?

Venus heard me sigh this song,
And by Loves sweetest Part, Variety, she swore,   20
She heard not this till now; and that it should be so no
    more.
She went, examin'd, and return'd ere long,
And said, alas, Some two or three
Poore Heretiques in love there bee,
Which thinke to stablish dangerous constancie.
But I have told them, since you will be true,
You shall be true to them, who'are false to you.

Loves Usury

For every houre that thou wilt spare mee now,
      I will allow,
Usurious God of Love, twenty to thee,
When with my browne, my gray haires equall bee;
Till then, Love, let my body raigne, and let
Mee travell, sojourne, snatch, plot, have, forget,
Resume my last yeares relict: thinke that yet
      We'had never met.

Let mee thinke any rivalls letter mine,
      And at next nine   10
Keepe midnights promise; mistake by the way
The maid, and tell the Lady of that delay;
Onely let mee love none, no, not the sport;
From country grasse, to comfitures of Court,
Or cities quelque choses, let report
      My minde transport.

This bargaine's good; if when I'am old, I bee
      Inflam'd by thee,
If thine owne honour, or my shame, or paine,
Thou covet most, at that age thou shalt gaine.   20
Doe thy will then, then subject and degree,
And fruit of love, Love I submit to thee,
Spare mee till then, I'll beare it, though she bee
      One that loves mee.

The Canonization

For Godsake hold your tongue, and let me love,
  Or chide my palsie, or my gout,
My five gray haires, or ruin'd fortune flout,
  With wealth your state, your minde with Arts improve,
    Take you a course, get you a place,
    Observe his honour, or his grace,
Or the Kings reall, or his stamped face

Contemplate, what you will, approve,
  So you will let me love.

Alas, alas, who's injur'd by my love?   10
  What merchants ships have my sighs drown'd?
Who saies my teares have overflow'd his ground?
  When did my colds a forward spring remove?
        When did the heats which my veines fill
        Adde one more to the plaguie Bill?
Soldiers finde warres, and Lawyers finde out still
  Litigious men, which quarrels move,
  Though she and I do love.

Call us what you will, wee are made such by love;
  Call her one, mee another flye,   20
We'are Tapers too, and at our owne cost die,
  And wee in us finde the'Eagle and the Dove.
        The Phœnix ridle hath more wit
        By us, we two being one, are it.
So to one neutrall thing both sexes fit,
  Wee dye and rise the same, and prove
  Mysterious by this love.

Wee can dye by it, if not live by love,
  And if unfit for tombes and hearse
Our legend bee, it will be fit for verse;   30
  And if no peece of Chronicle wee prove,
        We'll build in sonnets pretty roomes;
        As well a well wrought urne becomes
The greatest ashes, as halfe-acre tombes,
  And by these hymnes, all shall approve
  Us *Canoniz'd* for Love:

And thus invoke us; You whom reverend love
  Made one anothers hermitage;
You, to whom love was peace, that now is rage;
  Who did the whole worlds soule contract, and drove 40
        Into the glasses of your eyes
        So made such mirrors, and such spies,

[*The Canonization*] 33

That they did all to you epitomize,
    Countries, Townes, Courts: Beg from above
    A patterne of your love!

The triple Foole

    I am two fooles, I know,
For loving, and for saying so
    In whining Poëtry;
But where's that wiseman, that would not be I,
    If she would not deny?
Then as th'earths inward narrow crooked lanes
Do purge sea waters fretfull salt away,
    I thought, if I could draw my paines,
Through Rimes vexation, I should them allay,
Griefe brought to numbers cannot be so fierce,   10
For, he tames it, that fetters it in verse.

    But when I have done so,
Some man, his art and voice to show,
    Doth Set and sing my paine,
And, by delighting many, frees againe
    Griefe, which verse did restraine.
To Love, and Griefe tribute of Verse belongs,
But not of such as pleases when'tis read,
    Both are increased by such songs:
For both their triumphs so are published,   20
And I, which was two fooles, do so grow three;
Who are a little wise, the best fooles bee.

Lovers infinitenesse

If yet I have not all thy love,
Deare, I shall never have it all,
I cannot breath one other sigh, to move;
Nor can intreat one other teare to fall.
And all my treasure, which should purchase thee,

Sighs, teares, and oathes, and letters I have spent,
Yet no more can be due to mee,
Then at the bargaine made was ment,
If then thy gift of love were partiall,
That some to mee, some should to others fall,   10
  Deare, I shall never have Thee All.

Or if then thou gavest mee all,
All was but All, which thou hadst then,
But if in thy heart, since, there be or shall,
New love created bee, by other men,
Which have their stocks intire, and can in teares,
In sighs, in oathes, and letters outbid mee,
This new love may beget new feares,
For, this love was not vowed by thee.
And yet it was, thy gift being generall,   20
The ground, thy heart is mine, what ever shall
  Grow there, deare, I should have it all.

Yet I would not have all yet,
Hee that hath all can have no more,
And since my love doth every day admit
New growth, thou shouldst have new rewards in store;
Thou canst not every day give me thy heart,
If thou canst give it, then thou never gavest it:
Loves riddles are, that though thy heart depart,
It stayes at home, and thou with losing savest it: 30
But wee will have a way more liberall,
Then changing hearts, to joyne them, so wee shall
  Be one, and one anothers All.

Song

Sweetest love, I do not goe,
  For wearinesse of thee,
Nor in hope the world can show
  A fitter Love for mee;
    But since that I

Must dye at last, 'tis best,
To use my selfe in jest
   Thus by fain'd deaths to dye;

Yesternight the Sunne went hence,
   And yet is here to day,   10
He hath no desire nor sense,
   Nor halfe so short a way:
       Then feare not mee,
But beleeve that I shall make
Speedier journeyes, since I take
   More wings and spurres then hee.

O how feeble is mans power,
   That if good fortune fall,
Cannot adde another houre,
   Nor a lost houre recall!   20
       But come bad chance,
And wee joyne to'it our strength,
And wee teach it art and length,
   It selfe o'r us to'advance.

When thou sigh'st, thou sigh'st not winde,
   But sigh'st my soule away,
When thou weep'st, unkindly kinde,
   My lifes blood doth decay.
       It cannot bee
That thou lov'st mee, as thou say'st,   30
If in thine my life thou waste,
   Thou art the best of mee.

Let not thy divining heart
   Forethinke me any ill,
Destiny may take thy part,
   And may thy feares fulfill;
       But thinke that wee
Are but turn'd aside to sleepe;
They who one another keepe
   Alive, ne'r parted bee.   40

The Legacie

When I dyed last, and, Deare, I dye
  As often as from thee I goe,
  Though it be but an houre agoe,
And Lovers houres be full eternity,
I can remember yet, that I
  Something did say, and something did bestow;
Though I be dead, which sent mee, I should be
Mine owne executor and Legacie.

I heard mee say, Tell her anon,
  That my selfe, (that is you, not I,)   10
  Did kill me, and when I felt mee dye,
I bid mee send my heart, when I was gone,
But I alas could there finde none,
  When I had ripp'd me,'and search'd where hearts did
    lye;
It kill'd mee againe, that I who still was true,
In life, in my last Will should cozen you.

Yet I found something like a heart,
  But colours it, and corners had,
  It was not good, it was not bad,
It was intire to none, and few had part.   20
As good as could be made by art
  It seem'd; and therefore for our losses sad,
I meant to send this heart in stead of mine,
But oh, no man could hold it, for twas thine.

A Feaver

Oh doe not die, for I shall hate
  All women so, when thou art gone,
That thee I shall not celebrate,
  When I remember, thou wast one.

But yet thou canst not die, I know;
  To leave this world behinde, is death,

But when thou from this world wilt goe,
    The whole world vapors with thy breath.

Or if, when thou, the worlds soule, goest,
    It stay, tis but thy carkasse then,   10
The fairest woman, but thy ghost,
    But corrupt wormes, the worthyest men.

O wrangling schooles, that search what fire
    Shall burne this world, had none the wit
Unto this knowledge to aspire,
    That this her feaver might be it?

And yet she cannot wast by this,
    Nor long beare this torturing wrong,
For much corruption needful is
    To fuell such a feaver long.   20

These burning fits but meteors bee,
    Whose matter in thee is soone spent.
Thy beauty,'and all parts, which are thee,
    Are unchangeable firmament.

Yet t'was of my minde, seising thee,
    Though it in thee cannot persever.
For I had rather owner bee
    Of thee one houre, then all else ever.

Aire and Angels

Twice or thrice had I loved thee,
Before I knew thy face or name,
So in a voice, so in a shapelesse flame,
Angells affect us oft, and worship'd bee;
    Still when, to where thou wert, I came,
Some lovely glorious nothing I did see.
    But since my soule, whose child love is,
Takes limmes of flesh, and else could nothing doe,
    More subtile then the parent is,

Love must not be, but take a body too,   10
    And therefore what thou wert, and who,
        I bid Love aske, and now
That it assume thy body, I allow,
And fixe it selfe in thy lip, eye, and brow.

Whilst thus to ballast love, I thought,
And so more steddily to have gone,
With wares which would sinke admiration,
I saw, I had loves pinnace overfraught,
    Ev'ry thy haire for love to worke upon
Is much too much, some fitter must be sought;   20
    For, nor in nothing, nor in things
Extreme, and scatt'ring bright, can love inhere;
    Then as an Angell, face, and wings
Of aire, not pure as it, yet pure doth weare,
    So thy love may be my loves spheare;
        Just such disparitie
As is twixt Aire and Angells puritie,
'Twixt womens love, and mens will ever bee.

Breake of day

    'Tis true, 'tis day; what though it be?
    O wilt thou therefore rise from me?
Why should we rise, because 'tis light?
Did we lie downe, because 'twas night?
Love which in spight of darknesse brought us hether,
Should in despight of light keepe us together.

Light hath no tongue, but is all eye;
If it could speake as well as spie,
This were the worst, that it could say,
That being well, I faine would stay,   10
And that I lov'd my heart and honor so,
That I would not from him, that had them, goe.

Must businesse thee from hence remove?
Oh, that's the worst disease of love,

The poore, the foule, the false, love can
Admit, but not the busied man.
He which hath businesse, and makes love, doth doe
Such wrong, as when a maryed man doth wooe.

The Anniversarie

    All Kings, and all their favorites,
    All glory of honors, beauties, wits,
The Sun it selfe, which makes times, as they passe,
Is elder by a yeare, now, then it was
When thou and I first one another saw:
All other things, to their destruction draw,
    Only our love hath no decay;
This, no to morrow hath, nor yesterday,
Running it never runs from us away,
But truly keepes his first, last, everlasting day.   10

    Two graves must hide thine and my coarse,
    If one might, death were no divorce:
Alas, as well as other Princes, wee,
(Who Prince enough in one another bee,)
Must leave at last in death, these eyes, and eares,
Oft fed with true oathes, and with sweet salt teares;
    But soules where nothing dwells but love
(All other thoughts being inmates) then shall prove
This, or a love increased there above,
When bodies to their graves, soules from their graves re-
    move.   20

    And then wee shall be throughly blest,
    But wee no more, then all the rest;
Here upon earth, we'are Kings, and none but wee
Can be such Kings, nor of such subjects bee;
Who is so safe as wee? where none can doe
Treason to us, except one of us two.
    True and false feares let us refraine,

Let us love nobly, and live, and adde againe
Yeares and yeares unto yeares, till we attaine
To write threescore: this is the second of our raigne.   30

A Valediction: of my name, in the window

I

My name engrav'd herein,
Doth contribute my firmnesse to this glasse,
    Which, ever since that charme, hath beene
    As hard, as that which grav'd it, was;
Thine eye will give it price enough, to mock
        The diamonds of either rock.

II

        'Tis much that Glasse should bee
As all confessing, and through-shine as I,
    'Tis more, that it shewes thee to thee,
    And cleare reflects thee to thine eye.   10
But all such rules, loves magique can undoe,
        Here you see mee, and I am you.

III

        As no one point, nor dash,
Which are but accessaries to this name,
    The showers and tempests can outwash,
    So shall all times finde mee the same;
You this intirenesse better may fulfill,
        Who have the patterne with you still.

IV

        Or if too hard and deepe
This learning be, for a scratch'd name to teach,   20
    It, as a given deaths head keepe,
    Lovers mortalitie to preach,
Or thinke this ragged bony name to bee
        My ruinous Anatomie.

Then, as all my soules bee,
Emparadis'd in you, (in whom alone
  I understand, and grow and see,)
  The rafters of my body, bone
Being still with you, the Muscle, Sinew, and Veine,
      Which tile this house, will come againe: 30

VI

  Till my returne, repaire
And recompact my scattered body so.
  As all the vertuous powers which are
  Fix'd in the starres, are said to flow
Into such characters, as graved bee
      When these starres have supremacie:

VII

  So since this name was cut
When love and griefe their exaltation had,
  No doore 'gainst this names influence shut;
  As much more loving, as more sad,   40
'Twill make thee; and thou shouldst, till I returne,
      Since I die daily, daily mourne.

VIII

  When thy inconsiderate hand
Flings ope this casement, with my trembling name,
  To looke on one, whose wit or land,
  New battry to thy heart may frame,
Then thinke this name alive, and that thou thus
      In it offendst my Genius.

IX

  And when thy melted maid,
Corrupted by thy Lover's gold, and page,   50
  His letter at thy pillow'hath laid,
  Disputed it, and tam'd thy rage,
And thou begin'st to thaw towards him, for this,
      May my name step in, and hide his.

[A Valediction: of my name, in the window]   42

X

          And if this treason goe
To an overt act, and that thou write againe;
    In superscribing, this name flow
    Into thy fancy, from the pane.
So, in forgetting thou remembrest right,
          And unaware to mee shalt write.   60

XI

          But glasse, and lines must bee,
No meanes our firme substantiall love to keepe;
    Neere death inflicts this lethargie,
    And this I murmure in my sleepe;
Impute this idle talke, to that I goe,
          For dying men talke often so.

Twicknam garden

Blasted with sighs, and surrounded with teares,
    Hither I come to seeke the spring,
    And at mine eyes, and at mine eares,
Receive such balmes, as else cure every thing;
    But O, selfe traytor, I do bring
The spider love, which transubstantiates all,
    And can convert Manna to gall,
And that this place may thoroughly be thought
    True Paradise, I have the serpent brought.

'Twere wholsomer for mee, that winter did   10
    Benight the glory of this place,
    And that a grave frost did forbid
These trees to laugh, and mocke mee to my face;
    But that I may not this disgrace
Indure, nor yet leave loving, Love let mee
    Some senslesse peece of this place bee;
Make me a mandrake, so I may groane here,
    Or a stone fountaine weeping out my yeare.

Hither with christall vyals, lovers come,
   And take my teares, which are loves wine,   20
   And try your mistresse Teares at home,
For all are false, that tast not just like mine;
   Alas, hearts do not in eyes shine,
Nor can you more judge womans thoughts by teares,
   Then by her shadow, what she weares.
O perverse sexe, where none is true but shee,
   Who's therefore true, because her truth kills mee.

A Valediction: of the booke

I'll tell thee now (dear Love) what thou shalt doe
   To anger destiny, as she doth us,
   How I shall stay, though she Esloygne me thus,
And how posterity shall know it too;
      How thine may out-endure
      Sybills glory, and obscure
      Her who from Pindar could allure,
   And her, through whose helpe *Lucan* is not lame,
And her, whose booke (they say) *Homer* did finde,
   and name.

Study our manuscripts, those Myriades   10
   Of letters, which have past twixt thee and mee,
   Thence write our Annals, and in them will bee
To all whom loves subliming fire invades,
      Rule and example found;
      There, the faith of any ground
      No schismatique will dare to wound,
   That sees, how Love this grace to us affords,
To make, to keep, to use, to be these his Records.

This Booke, as long-liv'd as the elements,
   Or as the worlds forme, this all-graved tome   20
   In cypher writ, or new made Idiome,
Wee for loves clergie only'are instruments:
      When this booke is made thus,

Should againe the ravenous
Vandals and Goths inundate us,
Learning were safe; in this our Universe
Schooles might learne Sciences, Spheares Musick, Angels
Verse.

Here Loves Divines, (since all Divinity
Is love or wonder) may finde all they seeke,
Whether abstract spirituall love they like,   30
Their Soules exhal'd with what they do not see,
Or, loth so to amuze
Faiths infirmitie, they chuse
Something which they may see and use;
For, though minde be the heaven, where love doth sit,
Beauty a convenient type may be to figure it.

Here more then in their bookes may Lawyers finde,
Both by what titles Mistresses are ours,
And how prerogative these states devours,
Transferr'd from Love himselfe, to womankinde,   40
Who though from heart, and eyes,
They exact great subsidies,
Forsake him who on them relies,
And for the cause, honour, or conscience give,
Chimeraes, vaine as they, or their prerogative.

Here Statesmen, (or of them, they which can reade,)
May of their occupation finde the grounds:
Love and their art alike it deadly wounds,
If to consider what 'tis, one proceed,
In both they doe excell   50
Who the present governe well,
Whose weaknesse none doth, or dares tell;
In this thy booke, such will their nothing see,
As in the Bible some can finde out Alchimy.

Thus vent thy thoughts; abroad I'll studie thee,
As he removes farre off, that great heights takes;
How great love is, presence best tryall makes,

[A Valediction: of the booke]   45

But absence tryes how long this love will bee;
    To take a latitude
      Sun, or starres, are fitliest view'd   60
    At their brightest, but to conclude
Of longitudes, what other way have wee,
But to marke when, and where the darke eclipses bee?

Communitie

Good wee must love, and must hate ill,
For ill is ill, and good good still,
    But there are things indifferent,
Which wee may neither hate, nor love,
But one, and then another prove,
    As wee shall finde our fancy bent.

If then at first wise Nature had
Made women either good or bad,
    Then some wee might hate, and some chuse,
But since shee did them so create,   10
That we may neither love, nor hate,
    Onely this rests, All, all may use.

If they were good it would be seene,
Good is as visible as greene,
    And to all eyes it selfe betrayes:
If they were bad, they could not last,
Bad doth it selfe, and others wast,
    So, they deserve nor blame, nor praise.

But they are ours as fruits are ours,
He that but tasts, he that devours,   20
    And he that leaves all, doth as well:
Chang'd loves are but chang'd sorts of meat,
And when hee hath the kernell eate,
    Who doth not fling away the shell?

Loves growth

I scarce beleeve my love to be so pure
     As I had thought it was,
     Because it doth endure
Vicissitude, and season, as the grasse;
Me thinkes I lyed all winter, when I swore,
My love was infinite, if spring make'it more.

But if this medicine, love, which cures all sorrow
With more, not onely bee no quintessence,
But mixt of all stuffes, paining soule, or sense,
And of the Sunne his working vigour borrow,   10
Love's not so pure, and abstract, as they use
To say, which have no Mistresse but their Muse,
But as all else, being elemented too,
Love sometimes would contemplate, sometimes do.

And yet no greater, but more eminent,
     Love by the spring is growne;
     As, in the firmament,
Starres by the Sunne are not inlarg'd, but showne.
Gentle love deeds, as blossomes on a bough,
From loves awakened root do bud out now.   20

If, as in water stir'd more circles bee
Produc'd by one, love such additions take,
Those like so many spheares, but one heaven make,
For, they are all concentrique unto thee;
And though each spring doe adde to love new heate,
As princes doe in times of action get
New taxes, and remit them not in peace,
No winter shall abate the springs encrease.

Loves exchange

Love, any devill else but you,
Would for a given Soule give something too.
At Court your fellowes every day,

[Loves exchange]   47

Give th'art of Riming, Huntsmanship, or Play,
For them which were their owne before;
Onely I have nothing which gave more,
But am, alas, by being lowly, lower.

I aske no dispensation now
To falsifie a teare, or sigh, or vow,
I do not sue from thee to draw   10
A *non obstante* on natures law,
These are prerogatives, they inhere
In thee and thine; none should forsweare
Except that hee *Loves* minion were.

Give mee thy weaknesse, make mee blinde,
Both wayes, as thou and thine, in eies and minde;
Love, let me never know that this
Is Love, or, that love childish is;
Let me not know that others know
That she knowest my paines, least that so   20
A tender shame make me mine owne new woe.

If thou give nothing, yet thou'art just,
Because I would not thy first motions trust;
Small townes which stand stiffe, till great shot
Enforce them, by warres law *condition* not.
Such in loves warfare is my case,
I may not article for grace,
Having put Love at last to shew this face.

This face, by which he could command
And change the Idolatrie of any land,   30
This face, which wheresoe'r it comes,
Can call vow'd men from cloisters, dead from tombes,
And melt both Poles at once, and store
Deserts with cities, and make more
Mynes in the earth, then Quarries were before.

For this, Love is enrag'd with mee,
Yet kills not. If I must example bee
To future Rebells; If th'unborne

Must learne, by my being cut up, and torne:
Kill, and dissect me, Love; for this   **40**
Torture against thine owne end is,
Rack't carcasses make ill Anatomies.

Confined Love

   Some man unworthy to be possessor
Of old or new love, himselfe being false or weake,
   Thought his paine and shame would be lesser,
If on womankind he might his anger wreake,
         And thence a law did grow,
         One might but one man know;
         But are other creatures so?

   Are Sunne, Moone, or Starres by law forbidden,
To smile where they list, or lend away their light?
   Are birds divorc'd, or are they chidden   **10**
If they leave their mate, or lie abroad a night?
         Beasts doe no joyntures lose
         Though they new lovers choose,
         But we are made worse then those.

   Who e'r rigg'd faire ship to lie in harbors,
And not to seeke new lands, or not to deale withall?
   Or built faire houses, set trees, and arbors,
Only to lock up, or else to let them fall?
         Good is not good, unlesse
         A thousand it possesse,   **20**
         But doth wast with greedinesse.

The Dreame

Deare love, for nothing lesse then thee
Would I have broke this happy dreame,
     It was a theame
For reason, much too strong for phantasie,
Therefore thou wakd'st me wisely; yet

My Dreame thou brok'st not, but continued'st it,
Thou art so truth, that thoughts of thee suffice,
To make dreames truths; and fables histories;
Enter these armes, for since thou thoughtst it best,
Not to dreame all my dreame, let's act the rest.   10

As lightning, or a Tapers light,
Thine eyes, and not thy noise wak'd mee;
              Yet I thought thee
(For thou lovest truth) an Angell, at first sight,
But when I saw thou sawest my heart,
And knew'st my thoughts, beyond an Angels art,
When thou knew'st what I dreamt, when thou
       knew'st when
Excesse of joy would wake me, and cam'st then,
I must confesse, it could not chuse but bee
Prophane, to thinke thee any thing but thee.   20

Comming and staying show'd thee, thee,
But rising makes me doubt, that now,
              Thou art not thou.
That love is weake, where feare's as strong as hee;
Tis not all spirit, pure, and brave,
If mixture it of *Feare, Shame, Honor,* have.
Perchance as torches, which must ready bee,
Men light and put out, so thou deal'st with mee,
Thou cam'st to kindle, goest to come; Then I
Will dreame that hope againe, but else would die.   30

A Valediction: of weeping

              Let me powre forth
My teares before thy face, whil'st I stay here,
For thy face coines them, and thy stampe they beare,
And by this Mintage they are something worth,
              For thus they bee
              Pregnant of thee;
Fruits of much griefe they are, emblemes of more,
When a teare falls, that thou falst which it bore,

So thou and I are nothing then, when on a divers
    shore.

            On a round ball   10
A workeman that hath copies by, can lay
An Europe, Afrique, and an Asia,
And quickly make that, which was nothing, *All*,
            So doth each teare,
            Which thee doth weare,
A globe, yea world by that impression grow,
Till thy teares mixt with mine doe overflow
This world, by waters sent from thee, my heaven dis-
    solved so.

            O more then Moone,
Draw not up seas to drowne me in thy spheare,   20
Weepe me not dead, in thine armes, but forbeare
To teach the sea, what it may doe too soone;
            Let not the winde
            Example finde,
To doe me more harme, then it purposeth;
Since thou and I sigh one anothers breath,
Who e'r sighes most, is cruellest, and hasts the others
    death.

Loves Alchymie

Some that have deeper digg'd loves Myne then I,
Say, where his centrique happinesse doth lie:
        I have lov'd, and got, and told,
But should I love, get, tell, till I were old,
I should not finde that hidden mysterie;
        Oh, 'tis imposture all:
And as no chymique yet th'Elixar got,
        But glorifies his pregnant pot,
        If by the way to him befall
Some odoriferous thing, or medicinall,   10
    So, lovers dreame a rich and long delight,
    But get a winter-seeming summers night.

                              [*Loves Alchymie*]   51

Our ease, our thrift, our honor, and our day,
Shall we, for this vaine Bubles shadow pay?
    Ends love in this, that my man,
Can be as happy'as I can; If he can
Endure the short scorne of a Bridegroomes play?
    That loving wretch that sweares,
'Tis not the bodies marry, but the mindes,
    Which he in her Angelique findes,   20
    Would sweare as justly, that he heares,
In that dayes rude hoarse minstralsey, the spheares.
  Hope not for minde in women; at their best
  Sweetnesse and wit, they'are but *Mummy*, possest.

The Flea

Marke but this flea, and marke in this,
How little that which thou deny'st me is;
It suck'd me first, and now sucks thee,
And in this flea, our two bloods mingled bee;
Thou know'st that this cannot be said
A sinne, nor shame, nor losse of maidenhead,
  Yet this enjoyes before it wooe,
  And pamper'd swells with one blood made of two,
  And this, alas, is more then wee would doe.

Oh stay, three lives in one flea spare,   10
Where wee almost, yea more than maryed are,
This flea is you and I, and this
Our mariage bed, and mariage temple is;
Though parents grudge, and you, w'are met,
And cloysterd in these living walls of Jet.
  Though use make you apt to kill mee,
  Let not to that, selfe murder added bee,
  And sacrilege, three sinnes in killing three.

Cruell and sodaine, hast thou since
Purpled thy naile, in blood of innocence?   20
Wherein could this flea guilty bee,
Except in that drop which it suckt from thee?

Yet thou triumph'st, and saist that thou
Find'st not thy selfe, nor mee the weaker now;
   'Tis true, then learne how false, feares bee;
    Just so much honor, when thou yeeld'st to mee,
    Will wast, as this flea's death tooke life from thee.

The Curse

Who ever guesses, thinks, or dreames he knowes
Who is my mistris, wither by this curse;
       His only, and only his purse
      May some dull heart to love dispose,
And shee yeeld then to all that are his foes;
   May he be scorn'd by one, whom all else scorne,
   Forsweare to others, what to her he'hath sworne,
   With feare of missing, shame of getting, torne:

Madnesse his sorrow, gout his cramp, may hee
Make, by but thinking, who hath made him such: 10
      And may he feele no touch
      Of conscience, but of fame, and bee
Anguish'd, not that 'twas sinne, but that 'twas shee:
   In early and long scarcenesse may he rot,
   For land which had been his, if he had not
   Himself incestuously an heire begot:

May he dreame Treason, and beleeve, that hee
Meant to performe it, and confesse, and die,
      And no record tell why:
      His sonnes, which none of his may bee,   20
Inherite nothing but his infamie:
   Or may he so long Parasites have fed,
   That he would faine be theirs, whom he hath bred,
   And at the last be circumcis'd for bread:

The venom of all stepdames, gamsters gall,
What Tyrans, and their subjects interwish,
      What Plants, Mynes, Beasts, Foule, Fish,
      Can contribute, all ill which all

Prophets, or Poets spake; And all which shall
   Be annex'd in schedules unto this by mee,   30
Fall on that man; For if it be a shee
Nature before hand hath out-cursed mee.

The Message

Send home my long strayd eyes to mee,
Which (Oh) too long have dwelt on thee;
Yet since there they have learn'd such ill,
      Such forc'd fashions,
      And false passions,
         That they be
         Made by thee
Fit for no good sight, keep them still.

Send home my harmlesse heart againe,
Which no unworthy thought could staine;   10
But if it be taught by thine
      To make jestings
      Of protestings,
         And crosse both
         Word and oath,
Keepe it, for then 'tis none of mine.

Yet send me back my heart and eyes,
That I may know, and see thy lyes,
And may laugh and joy, when thou
      Art in anguish   20
      And dost languish
         For some one
         That will none,
Or prove as false as thou art now.

A nocturnall upon S. Lucies day,

Being the shortest day

Tis the yeares midnight, and it is the dayes,
Lucies, who scarce seaven houres herself unmaskes,
  The Sunne is spent, and now his flasks
  Send forth light squibs, no constant rayes;
      The worlds whole sap is sunke:
The generall balme th'hydroptique earth hath drunk,
Whither, as to the beds-feet, life is shrunke,
Dead and enterr'd; yet all these seeme to laugh,
Compar'd with mee, who am their Epitaph.

Study me then, you who shall lovers bee   10
At the next world, that is, at the next Spring:
  For I am every dead thing,
  In whom love wrought new Alchimie.
      For his art did expresse
A quintessence even from nothingnesse,
From dull privations, and leane emptinesse:
He ruin'd mee, and I am re-begot
Of absence, darknesse, death; things which are not.

All others, from all things, draw all that's good,
Life, soule, forme, spirit, whence they beeing have;   20
  I, by loves limbecke, am the grave
  Of all, that's nothing. Oft a flood
      Have wee two wept, and so
Drownd the whole world, us two; oft did we grow
To be two Chaosses, when we did show
Care to ought else; and often absences
Withdrew our soules, and made us carcasses.

But I am by her death, (which word wrongs her)
Of the first nothing, the Elixer grown;
  Were I a man, that I were one,   30
  I needs must know; I should preferre,
      If I were any beast,
Some ends, some means; Yea plants, yea stones detest,
And love; All, all some properties invest;

If I an ordinary nothing were,
As shadow, a light, and body must be here.

But I am None; nor will my Sunne renew.
You lovers, for whose sake, the lesser Sunne
  At this time to the Goat is runne
    To fetch new lust, and give it you,   40
        Enjoy your summer all;
Since shee enjoyes her long nights festivall,
Let mee prepare towards her, and let mee call
This houre her Vigill, and her Eve, since this
Both the yeares, and the dayes deep midnight is.

Witchcraft by a picture

I fixe mine eye on thine, and there
  Pitty my picture burning in thine eye,
My picture drown'd in a transparent teare,
  When I looke lower I espie;
    Hadst thou the wicked skill
By pictures made and mard, to kill,
How many wayes mightst thou performe thy will?

But now I have drunke thy sweet salt teares,
  And though thou poure more I'll depart;
My picture vanish'd, vanish feares,   10
  That I can be endamag'd by that art;
    Though thou retaine of mee
One picture more, yet that will bee,
Being in thine owne heart, from all malice free.

The Baite

Come live with mee, and bee my love,
And we will some new pleasures prove
Of golden sands, and christall brookes,
With silken lines, and silver hookes.

There will the river whispering runne
Warm'd by thy eyes, more then the Sunne.
And there the'inamor'd fish will stay,
Begging themselves they may betray.

When thou wilt swimme in that live bath,
Each fish, which every channell hath,   10
Will amorously to thee swimme,
Gladder to catch thee, then thou him.

If thou, to be so seene, beest loath,
By Sunne, or Moone, thou darknest both,
And if my selfe have leave to see,
I need not their light, having thee.

Let others freeze with angling reeds,
And cut their legges, with shells and weeds,
Or treacherously poore fish beset,
With strangling snare, or windowie net: 20

Let coarse bold hands, from slimy nest
The bedded fish in banks out-wrest,
Or curious traitors, sleavesilke flies
Bewitch poore fishes wandring eyes.

For thee, thou needst no such deceit,
For thou thy selfe art thine owne bait;
That fish, that is not catch'd thereby,
Alas, is wiser farre then I.

The Apparition

When by thy scorne, O murdresse, I am dead,
And that thou thinkst thee free
From all solicitation from mee,
Then shall my ghost come to thy bed,
And thee, fain'd vestall, in worse armes shall see;
Then thy sicke taper will begin to winke,

And he, whose thou art then, being tyr'd before,
Will, if thou stirre, or pinch to wake him, thinke
      Thou call'st for more,
And in false sleepe will from thee shrinke,   10
And then poore Aspen wretch, neglected thou
Bath'd in a cold quicksilver sweat wilt lye
      A veryer ghost then I;
What I will say, I will not tell thee now,
Lest that preserve thee'; and since my love is spent,
I'had rather thou shouldst painfully repent,
Then by my threatnings rest still innocent.

The broken heart

He is starke mad, who ever sayes,
   That he hath beene in love an houre,
Yet not that love so soone decayes,
   But that it can tenne in lesse space devour;
Who will beleeve mee, if I sweare
That I have had the plague a yeare?
   Who would not laugh at mee, if I should say,
   I saw a flaske of *powder burne a day*?

Ah, what a trifle is a heart,
   If once into loves hands it come!   10
All other griefes allow a part
   To other griefes, and aske themselves but some;
They come to us, but us Love draws,
Hee swallows us, and never chawes:
   By him, as by chain'd shot, whole rankes doe dye,
   He is the tyran Pike, our hearts the Frye.

If 'twere not so, what did become
   Of my heart, when I first saw thee?
I brought a heart into the roome,
   But from the roome, I carried none with mee: 20
If it had gone to thee, I know
Mine would have taught thine heart to show

More pitty unto mee: but Love, alas,
   At one first blow did shiver it as glasse.

Yet nothing can to nothing fall,
   Nor any place be empty quite,
Therefore I thinke my breast hath all
   Those peeces still, though they be not unite;
And now as broken glasses show
A hundred lesser faces, so   30
   My ragges of heart can like, wish, and adore,
   But after one such love, can love no more.

A Valediction: forbidding mourning

As virtuous men passe mildly away,
   And whisper to their soules, to goe,
Whilst some of their sad friends doe say,
   The breath goes now, and some say, no:

So let us melt, and make no noise,
   No teare-floods, nor sigh-tempests move,
T'were prophanation of our joyes
   To tell the layetie our love.

Moving of th'earth brings harmes and feares,
   Men reckon what it did and meant,   10
But trepidation of the spheares,
   Though greater farre, is innocent.

Dull sublunary lovers love
   (Whose soule is sense) cannot admit
Absence, because it doth remove
   Those things which elemented it.

But we by a love, so much refin'd,
   That our selves know not what it is,
Inter-assured of the mind,
   Care lesse, eyes, lips, and hands to misse.   20

Our two soules therefore, which are one,
　　Though I must goe, endure not yet
A breach, but an expansion,
　　Like gold to ayery thinnesse beate.

If they be two, they are two so
　　As stiffe twin compasses are two,
Thy soule the fixt foot, makes no show
　　To move, but doth, if the'other doe.

And though it in the center sit,
　　Yet when the other far doth rome, 　　　　　　30
It leanes, and hearkens after it,
　　And growes erect, as that comes home.

Such wilt thou be to mee, who must
　　Like th'other foot, obliquely runne;
Thy firmnes makes my circle just,
　　And makes me end, where I begunne.

The Extasie

Where, like a pillow on a bed,
　　A Pregnant banke swel'd up, to rest
The violets reclining head,
　　Sat we two, one anothers best.
Our hands were firmely cimented
　　With a fast balme, which thence did spring,
Our eye-beames twisted, and did thred
　　Our eyes, upon one double string;
So to'entergraft our hands, as yet
　　Was all the meanes to make us one, 　　　　　　10
And pictures in our eyes to get
　　Was all our propagation.
As 'twixt two equal Armies, Fate
　　Suspends uncertaine victorie,
Our soules, (which to advance their state,
　　Were gone out,) hung 'twixt her, and mee.

And whil'st our soules negotiate there,
  Wee like sepulchrall statues lay;
All day, the same our postures were,
  And wee said nothing, all the day.   20
If any, so by love refin'd,
  That he soules language understood,
And by good love were growen all minde,
  Within convenient distance stood,
He (though he knew not which soule spake,
  Because both meant, both spake the same)
Might thence a new concoction take,
  And part farre purer then he came.
This Extasie doth unperplex
  (We said) and tell us what we love,   30
Wee see by this, it was not sexe,
  Wee see, we saw not what did move:
But as all severall soules containe
  Mixture of things, they know not what,
Love, these mixt soules doth mixe againe,
  And makes both one, each this and that.
A single violet transplant,
  The strength, the colour, and the size,
(All which before was poore, and scant,)
  Redoubles still, and multiplies.   40
When love, with one another so
  Interinanimates two soules,
That abler soule, which thence doth flow,
  Defects of lonelinesse controules.
Wee then, who are this new soule, know,
  Of what we are compos'd, and made,
For, th'Atomies of which we grow,
  Are soules, whom no change can invade.
But O alas, so long, so farre
  Our bodies why doe wee forbeare?   50
They'are ours, though they'are not wee, Wee are
  The intelligences, they the spheare.
We owe them thankes, because they thus,
  Did us, to us, at first convay,
Yeelded their forces, sense, to us,

Nor are drosse to us, but allay.
On man heavens influence workes not so,
    But that it first imprints the ayre,
Soe soule into the soule may flow,
    Though it to body first repaire.   60
As our blood labours to beget
    Spirits, as like soules as it can,
Because such fingers need to knit
    That subtile knot, which makes us man:
So must pure lovers soules descend
    T'affections, and to faculties,
Which sense may reach and apprehend,
    Else a great Prince in prison lies.
To'our bodies turne wee then, that so
    Weake men on love reveal'd may looke;   70
Loves mysteries in soules doe grow,
    But yet the body is his booke.
And if some lover, such as wee,
    Have heard this dialogue of one,
Let him still marke us, he shall see
    Small change, when we'are to bodies gone.

Loves Deitie

I long to talke with some old lovers ghost,
    Who dyed before the god of Love was borne:
I cannot thinke that hee, who then lov'd most,
    Sunke so low, as to love one which did scorne.
But since this god produc'd a destinie,
And that vice-nature, custome, lets it be;
    I must love her, that loves not mee.

Sure, they which made him god, meant not so much,
    Nor he, in his young godhead practis'd it;
But when an even flame two hearts did touch,   10
    His office was indulgently to fit
Actives to passives. Correspondencie
Only his subject was; It cannot bee
    Love, till I love her, that loves mee.

But every moderne god will now extend
  His vast prerogative, as far as Jove.
To rage, to lust, to write to, to commend,
  All is the purlewe of the God of Love.
Oh were wee wak'ned by this Tyrannie
To ungod this child againe, it could not bee   20
  I should love her, who loves not mee.

Rebell and Atheist too, why murmure I,
  As though I felt the worst that love could doe?
Love might make me leave loving, or might trie
  A deeper plague, to make her love me too,
Which, since she loves before, I'am loth to see;
Falshood is worse then hate; and that must bee,
  If shee whom I love, should love mee.

Loves diet

To what a combersome unwieldinesse
And burdenous corpulence my love had growne,
  But that I did, to make it lesse,
  And keepe it in proportion,
Give it a diet, made it feed upon
That which love worst endures, *discretion*.

Above one sigh a day I'allow'd him not,
Of which my fortune, and my faults had part;
  And if sometimes by stealth he got
  A she sigh from my mistresse heart,   10
And thought to feast on that, I let him see
'Twas neither very sound, nor meant to mee.

If he wroung from mee'a teare, I brin'd it so
With scorne or shame, that him it nourish'd not;
  If he suck'd hers, I let him know
  'Twas not a teare, which hee had got,
His drinke was counterfeit, as was his meat;
For, eyes which rowle towards all, weepe not, but sweat.

What ever he would dictate, I writ that,
But burnt my letters; When she writ to me,   20
   And that that favour made him fat,
    I said, if any title bee
Convey'd by this, Ah, what doth it availe,
To be the fortieth name in an entaile?

Thus I reclaim'd my buzard love, to flye
At what, and when, and how, and where I chuse;
   Now negligent of sport I lye,
    And now as other Fawkners use,
I spring a mistresse, sweare, write, sigh and weepe:
And the game kill'd, or lost, goe talke, and sleepe.   30

The Will

    Before I sigh my last gaspe, let me breath,
    Great love, some Legacies; Here I bequeath
    Mine eyes to *Argus*, if mine eyes can see,
    If they be blinde, then Love, I give them thee;
    My tongue to Fame; to'Embassadours mine eares;
      To women or the sea, my teares.
    Thou, Love, hast taught mee heretofore
  By making mee serve her who'had twenty more,
That I should give to none, but such, as had too much
    before.

    My constancie I to the planets give;   10
    My truth to them, who at the Court doe live;
    Mine ingenuity and opennesse,
    To Jesuites; to Buffones my pensivenesse;
    My silence to'any, who abroad hath beene;
      My mony to a Capuchin.
    Thou Love taught'st me, by appointing mee
  To love there, where no love receiv'd can be,
Onely to give to such as have an incapacitie.

    My faith I give to Roman Catholiques;
    All my good works unto the Schismaticks   20

Of Amsterdam; my best civility
And Courtship, to an Universitie;
My modesty I give to souldiers bare;
   My patience let gamesters share.
Thou Love taughtst mee, by making mee
Love her that holds my love disparity,
Onely to give to those that count my gifts indignity.

I give my reputation to those
Which were my friends; Mine industrie to foes;
To Schoolemen I bequeath my doubtfulnesse; 30
My sicknesse to Physitians, or excesse;
To Nature, all that I in Ryme have writ;
   And to my company my wit.
Thou Love, by making mee adore
Her, who begot this love in mee before,
Taughtst me to make, as though I gave, when I did but
   restore.

To him for whom the passing bell next tolls,
I give my physick bookes; my writen rowles
Of Morall counsels, I to Bedlam give;
My brazen medals, unto them which live 40
In want of bread; To them which passe among
   All forrainers, mine English tongue.
Thou, Love, by making mee love one
Who thinkes her friendship a fit portion
For yonger lovers, dost my gifts thus disproportion.

Therefore I'll give no more; But I'll undoe
The world by dying; because love dies too.
Then all your beauties will bee no more worth
Then gold in Mines, where none doth draw it forth;
And all your graces no more use shall have 50
   Then a Sun dyall in a grave.
Thou Love taughtst mee, by making mee
Love her, who doth neglect both mee and thee,
To'invent, and practise this one way, to'annihilate all
   three.

The Funerall

Who ever comes to shroud me, do not harme
    Nor question much
That subtile wreath of haire, which crowns my arme;
The mystery, the signe you must not touch,
    For 'tis my outward Soule,
Viceroy to that, which then to heaven being gone,
    Will leave this to controule,
And keepe these limbes, her Provinces, from dissolution.

For if the sinewie thread my braine lets fall
    Through every part,   10
Can tye those parts, and make mee one of all;
These haires which upward grew, and strength and art
    Have from a better braine,
Can better do'it; Except she meant that I
    By this should know my pain,
As prisoners then are manacled, when they'are condemn'd
    to die.

What ere shee meant by'it, bury it with me,
    For since I am
Loves martyr, it might breed idolatrie,
If into others hands these Reliques came;   20
    As 'twas humility
To afford to it all that a Soule can doe,
    So, 'tis some bravery,
That since you would save none of mee, I bury some of
    you.

The Blossome

  Little think'st thou, poore flower,
  Whom I have watch'd sixe or seaven dayes,
And seene thy birth, and seene what every houre
Gave to thy growth, thee to this height to raise,
And now dost laugh and triumph on this bough,

                Little think'st thou
That it will freeze anon, and that I shall
To morrow finde thee falne, or not at all.

    Little think'st thou poore heart
        That labour'st yet to nestle thee,
And think'st by hovering here to get a part
In a forbidden or forbidding tree,
And hop'st her stiffenesse by long siege to bow:
                Little think'st thou,
That thou to morrow, ere that Sunne doth wake,
Must with this Sunne, and mee a journey take.

    But thou which lov'st to bee
        Subtile to plague thy selfe, wilt say,
Alas, if you must goe, what's that to mee?
Here lyes my businesse, and here I will stay:
You goe to friends, whose love and meanes present
                Various content
To your eyes, eares, and tongue, and every part.
If then your body goe, what need you a heart?

    Well then, stay here; but know,
        When thou hast stayd and done thy most;
A naked thinking heart, that makes no show,
Is to a woman, but a kinde of Ghost;
How shall shee know my heart; or having none,
                Know thee for one?
Practise may make her know some other part,
But take my word, shee doth not know a Heart.

    Meet mee at London, then,
        Twenty dayes hence, and thou shalt see
Mee fresher, and more fat, by being with men,
Then if I had staid still with her and thee.
For Gods sake, if you can, be you so too:
                I would give you
There, to another friend, whom wee shall finde
As glad to have my body, as my minde.

The Primrose, being at Mountgomery Castle, upon the hill, on which it is situate

Upon this Primrose hill,
    Where, if Heav'n would distill
A shoure of raine, each severall drop might goe
To his owne primrose, and grow Manna so;
And where their forme, and their infinitie
    Make a terrestriall Galaxie,
    As the small starres doe in the skie:
I walke to finde a true Love; and I see
That 'tis not a mere woman, that is shee,
But must, or more, or lesse then woman bee.   10

    Yet know I not, which flower
    I wish; a sixe, or foure;
For should my true-Love lesse then woman bee,
She were scarce any thing; and then, should she
Be more then woman, shee would get above
    All thought of sexe, and thinke to move
    My heart to study her, and not to love;
Both these were monsters; Since there must reside
Falshood in woman, I could more abide,
She were by art, then Nature falsify'd.   20

    Live Primrose then, and thrive
    With thy true number five;
And women, whom this flower doth represent,
With this mysterious number be content;
Ten is the farthest number; if halfe ten
    Belonge unto each woman, then
    Each woman may take halfe us men;
Or if this will not serve their turne, Since all
Numbers are odde, or even, and they fall
First into this, five, women may take us all.   30

When my grave is broke up againe
Some second ghest to entertaine,
(For graves have learn'd that woman-head
To be to more then one a Bed)
     And he that digs it, spies
A bracelet of bright haire about the bone,
     Will he not let'us alone,
And thinke that there a loving couple lies,
Who thought that this device might be some way
To make their soules, at the last busie day,   10
Meet at this grave, and make a little stay?

If this fall in a time, or land,
Where mis-devotion doth command,
Then, he that digges us up, will bring
Us, to the Bishop, and the King,
     To make us Reliques; then
Thou shalt be a Mary Magdalen, and I
     A something else thereby;
All women shall adore us, and some men;
And since at such time, miracles are sought,   20
I would have that age by this paper taught
What miracles wee harmelesse lovers wrought.

First, we lov'd well and faithfully,
Yet knew not what wee lov'd, nor why,
Difference of sex no more wee knew,
Then our Guardian Angells doe;
     Comming and going, wee
Perchance might kisse, but not between those meales;
     Our hands ne'r toucht the seales,
Which nature, injur'd by late law, sets free: 30
These miracles wee did; but now alas,
All measure, and all language, I should passe,
Should I tell what a miracle shee was.

The Dampe

When I am dead, and Doctors know not why,
      And my friends curiositie
Will have me cut up to survay each part,
When they shall finde your Picture in my heart,
      You thinke a sodaine dampe of love
      Will through all their senses move,
And worke on them as mee, and so preferre
Your murder, to the name of Massacre.

Poore victories! But if you dare be brave,
      And pleasure in your conquest have,   10
First kill th'enormous Gyant, your *Disdaine*,
And let th'enchantresse *Honor*, next be slaine,
      And like a Goth and Vandall rize,
      Deface Records, and Histories
Of your owne arts and triumphs over men,
And without such advantage kill me then.

For I could muster up as well as you
      My Gyants, and my Witches too,
Which are vast *Constancy*, and *Secretnesse*,
But these I neyther looke for, nor professe;   20
      Kill mee as Woman, let mee die
      As a meere man; doe you but try
Your passive valor, and you shall finde than,
Naked you'have odds enough of any man.

The Dissolution

Shee'is dead; And all which die
  To their first Elements resolve;
And wee were mutuall Elements to us,
  And made of one another.
  My body then doth hers involve,
And those things whereof I consist, hereby
In me abundant grow, and burdenous,
    And nourish not, but smother.

My fire of Passion, sighes of ayre,
Water of teares, and earthly sad despaire,   10
      Which my materialls bee,
But neere worne out by loves securitie,
Shee, to my losse, doth by her death repaire,
   And I might live long wretched so
But that my fire doth with my fuell grow.
     Now as those Active Kings
  Whose foraine conquest treasure brings,
Receive more, and spend more, and soonest breake:
This (which I am amaz'd that I can speake)
     This death, hath with my store   20
       My use encreas'd.
And so my soule more earnestly releas'd,
Will outstrip hers; As bullets flowen before
A latter bullet may o'rtake, the pouder being more.

A Jeat Ring sent

    Thou art not so black, as my heart,
  Nor halfe so brittle, as her heart, thou art;
What would'st thou say? shall both our properties by thee
    bee spoke,
  Nothing more endlesse, nothing sooner broke?

    Marriage rings are not of this stuffe;
  Oh, why should ought lesse precious, or lesse tough
Figure our loves? Except in thy name thou have bid it say,
  I'am cheap, and nought but fashion, fling me'away.

    Yet stay with mee since thou art come,
  Circle this fingers top, which did'st her thombe.   10
Be justly proud, and gladly safe, that thou dost dwell with
    me,
  She that, Oh, broke her faith, would soon breake thee.

Negative love

I never stoop'd so low, as they
Which on an eye, cheeke, lip, can prey,
   Seldome to them, which soare no higher
   Then vertue or the minde to'admire,
For sense, and understanding may
   Know, what gives fuell to their fire:
My love, though silly, is more brave,
For may I misse, when ere I crave,
If I know yet, what I would have.

If that be simply perfectest   10
Which can by no way be exprest
   But *Negatives*, my love is so.
   To All, which all love, I say no.
If any who deciphers best,
   What we know not, our selves, can know,
Let him teach mee that nothing; This
As yet my ease, and comfort is,
Though I speed not, I cannot misse.

The Prohibition

      Take heed of loving mee,
At least remember, I forbade it thee;
Not that I shall repaire my'unthrifty wast
Of Breath and Blood, upon thy sighes, and teares,
By being to thee then what to me thou wast;
But, so great Joy, our life at once outweares,
Then, least thy love, by my death, frustrate bee,
If thou love mee, take heed of loving mee.

      Take heed of hating mee,
Or too much triumph in the Victorie.   10
Not that I shall be mine owne officer,
And hate with hate againe retaliate;
But thou wilt lose the stile of conquerour,

If I, thy conquest, perish by thy hate.
Then, least my being nothing lessen thee,
If thou hate mee, take heed of hating mee.

        Yet, love and hate mee too,
So, these extreames shall neithers office doe;
Love mee, that I may die the gentler way;
Hate mee, because thy love'is too great for mee;   20
Or let these two, themselves, not me decay;
So shall I, live, thy Stage, not triumph bee;
Lest thou thy love and hate and mee undoe,
To let mee live, O love and hate mee too.

The Expiration

So, so, breake off this last lamenting kisse,
    Which sucks two soules, and vapors Both away,
Turne thou ghost that way, and let mee turne this,
    And let our selves benight our happiest day,
We ask'd none leave to love; nor will we owe
    Any, so cheape a death, as saying, Goe;

Goe; and if that word have not quite kil'd thee,
    Ease mee with death, by bidding mee goe too.
Or, if it have, let my word worke on mee,
    And a just office on a murderer doe.   10
Except it be too late, to kill me so,
    Being double dead, going, and bidding, goe.

The Computation

For the first twenty yeares, since yesterday,
    I scarce beleev'd, thou could'st be gone away,
For forty more, I fed on favours past,
    And forty'on hopes, that thou would'st, they might last.
Teares drown'd one hundred, and sighes blew out two,
    A thousand, I did neither thinke, nor doe,

Or not divide, all being one thought of you;
Or in a thousand more, forgot that too.
Yet call not this long life; But thinke that I
Am, by being dead, Immortall; Can ghosts die?   10

The Paradox

No Lover saith, I love, nor any other
      Can judge a perfect Lover;
Hee thinkes that else none can, nor will agree
      That any loves but hee:
I cannot say I lov'd, for who can say
      Hee was kill'd yesterday?
Love with excesse of heat, more yong then old,
      Death kills with too much cold;
Wee dye but once, and who lov'd last did die,
      Hee that saith twice, doth lye: 10
For though hee seeme to move, and stirre a while,
      It doth the sense beguile.
Such life is like the light which bideth yet
      When the lights life is set,
Or like the heat, which fire in solid matter
      Leaves behinde, two houres after.
Once I lov'd and dy'd; and am now become
      Mine Epitaph and Tombe.
Here dead men speake their last, and so do I;
      Love-slaine, loe, here I lye.   20

Farewell to love

      Whilst yet to prove,
I thought there was some Deitie in love
   So did I reverence, and gave
Worship, as Atheists at their dying houre
Call, what they cannot name, an unknowne power,
   As ignorantly did I crave:
        Thus when
Things not yet knowne are coveted by men,

Our desires give them fashion, and so
As they waxe lesser, fall, as they rise, grow.   10

            But, from late faire
His highnesse sitting in a golden Chaire,
    Is not lesse cared for after three dayes
By children, then the thing which lovers so
Blindly admire, and with such worship wooe;
    Being had, enjoying it decayes:
                And thence,
What before pleas'd them all, takes but one sense,
    And that so lamely, as it leaves behinde
A kinde of sorrowing dulnesse to the minde.   20

            Ah cannot wee,
As well as Cocks and Lyons jocund be,
    After such pleasures? Unlesse wise
Nature decreed (since each such Act, they say,
Diminisheth the length of life a day)
    This, as shee would man should despise
                The sport;
Because that other curse of being short,
    And onely for a minute made to be
Eager, desires to raise posterity.   30

            Since so, my minde
Shall not desire what no man else can finde,
    I'll no more dote and runne
To pursue things which had indammag'd me.
And when I come where moving beauties be,
    As men doe when the summers Sunne
                Growes great,
Though I admire their greatnesse, shun their heat;
    Each place can afford shadowes. If all faile,
'Tis but applying worme-seed to the Taile.   40

A Lecture upon the Shadow

Stand still, and I will read to thee
A Lecture, Love, in loves philosophy.
      These three houres that we have spent,
      Walking here, Two shadowes went
Along with us, which we our selves produc'd;
But, now the Sunne is just above our head,
      We doe those shadowes tread;
      And to brave clearnesse all things are reduc'd.
  So whilst our infant loves did grow,
  Disguises did, and shadowes, flow,   10
  From us, and our cares; but, now 'tis not so.

That love hath not attain'd the high'st degree,
Which is still diligent lest others see.

Except our loves at this noone stay,
We shall new shadowes make the other way.
      As the first were made to blinde
      Others; these which come behinde
Will worke upon our selves, and blind our eyes.
If our loves faint, and westwardly decline;
      To me thou, falsly, thine,   20
      And I to thee mine actions shall disguise.
  The morning shadowes weare away,
  But these grow longer all the day,
  But oh, loves day is short, if love decay.

Love is growing, or full constant light;
And his first minute, after noone, is night.

A lame begger

I am unable, yonder begger cries,
To stand, or move; if he say true, hee *lies*.

A selfe accuser

Your mistris, that you follow whores, still taxeth you:
'Tis strange that she should thus confesse it, though'it be
    true.

A licentious person

Thy sinnes and haires may no man equall call,
For, as thy sinnes increase, thy haires doe fall.

Antiquary

If in his Studie he hath so much care
To'hang all old strange things, let his wife beware.

Phryne

Thy flattering picture, *Phryne*, is like thee,
Onely in this, that you both painted be.

Klockius

Klockius so deeply hath sworne, ne'r more to come
In bawdie house, that hee dares not goe home.

Raderus

Why this man gelded *Martiall* I muse,
Except himselfe alone his tricks would use,
As *Katherine*, for the Courts sake, put downe Stewes.

i *Jealosie*

Fond woman, which would'st have thy husband die,
And yet complain'st of his great jealousie;
If swolne with poyson, hee lay in'his last bed,
His body with a sere-barke covered,
Drawing his breath, as thick and short, as can
The nimblest crocheting Musitian,
Ready with loathsome vomiting to spue
His Soule out of one hell, into a new,
Made deafe with his poore kindreds howling cries,
Begging with few feign'd teares, great legacies,   10
Thou would'st not weepe, but jolly,'and frolicke bee,
As a slave, which to morrow should be free;
Yet weep'st thou, when thou seest him hungerly
Swallow his owne death, hearts-bane jealousie.
O give him many thanks, he'is courteous,
That in suspecting kindly warneth us.
Wee must not, as wee us'd, flout openly,
In scoffing ridles, his deformitie;
Nor at his boord together being satt,
With words, nor touch, scarce lookes adulterate.   20
Nor when he swolne, and pamper'd with great fare,
Sits downe, and snorts, cag'd in his basket chaire,
Must wee usurpe his owne bed any more,
Nor kisse and play in his house, as before.
Now I see many dangers; for that is
His realme, his castle, and his diocesse.
But if, as envious men, which would revile
Their Prince, or coyne his gold, themselves exile
Into another countrie,'and doe it there,
Wee play'in another house, what should we feare?   30
There we will scorne his houshold policies,
His seely plots, and pensionary spies,
As the inhabitants of Thames right side
Do Londons Major; or Germans, the Popes pride.

vii   "Natures lay Ideot"

Natures lay Ideot, I taught thee to love,
And in that sophistrie, Oh, thou dost prove
Too subtile: Foole, thou didst not understand
The mystique language of the eye nor hand:
Nor couldst thou judge the difference of the aire
Of sighes, and say, this lies, this sounds despaire:
Nor by the'eyes water call a maladie
Desperately hot, or changing feaverously.
I had not taught thee then, the Alphabet
Of flowers, how they devisefully being set   10
And bound up, might with speechlesse secrecie
Deliver errands mutely, and mutually.
Remember since all thy words us'd to bee
To every suitor; *I, if my friends agree;*
Since, household charmes, thy husbands name to teach,
Were all the love trickes, that thy wit could reach;
And since, an houres discourse could scarce have made
One answer in thee, and that ill arraid
In broken proverbs, and torne sentences.
Thou art not by so many duties his,   20
That from the worlds Common having sever'd thee,
Inlaid thee, neither to be seene, nor see,
As mine: who have with amorous delicacies
Refin'd thee'into a blis-full Paradise.
Thy graces and good words my creatures bee;
I planted knowledge and lifes tree in thee,
Which Oh, shall strangers taste? Must I alas
Frame and enamell Plate, and drinke in Glasse?
Chafe waxe for others seales? breake a colts force
And leave him then, beeing made a ready horse?   30

ix   The Autumnall

No *Spring,* nor *Summer* Beauty hath such grace,
    As I have seen in one *Autumnall* face.
Yong *Beauties* force our love, and that's a *Rape,*
    This doth but *counsaile,* yet you cannot scape.

If t'were a *shame* to love, here t'were no *shame*,
    Affection here takes *Reverences* name.
Were her first yeares the *Golden Age;* That's true,
    But now shee's *gold* oft tried, and ever new.
That was her torrid and inflaming time,
    This is her tolerable *Tropique clyme*.   10
Faire eyes, who askes more heate then comes from hence,
    He in a fever wishes pestilence.
Call not these wrinkles, *graves;* If *graves* they were,
    They were *Loves graves;* for else he is no where.
Yet lies not Love *dead* here, but here doth sit
    Vow'd to this trench, like an *Anachorit*.
And here, till hers, which must be his *death,* come,
    He doth not digge a *Grave,* but build a *Tombe*.
Here dwells he, though he sojourne ev'ry where,
    In *Progresse,* yet his standing house is here.   20
Here, where still *Evening* is; not *noone,* nor *night;*
    Where no *voluptuousnesse,* yet all *delight*.
In all her words, unto all hearers fit,
    You may at *Revels,* you at *Counsaile,* sit.
This is loves timber, youth his under-wood;
    There he, as wine in *June,* enrages blood,
Which then comes seasonabliest, when our tast
    And appetite to other things, is past.
Xerxes strange *Lydian* love, the *Platane* tree,
    Was lov'd for age, none being so large as shee,   30
Or else because, being yong, nature did blesse
    Her youth with ages glory, *Barrennesse*.
If we love things long sought, *Age* is a thing
    Which we are fifty yeares in compassing.
If transitory things, which soone decay,
    Age must be lovelyest at the latest day.
But name not *Winter-faces,* whose skin's slacke;
    Lanke, as an unthrifts purse; but a soules sacke;
Whose *Eyes* seeke light within, for all here's shade;
    Whose *mouthes* are holes, rather worne out, then made;
Whose every tooth to a severall place is gone,   41
    To vexe their soules at *Resurrection;*
Name not these living *Deaths-heads* unto mee,
    For these, not *Ancient,* but *Antique* be.

I hate extreames; yet I had rather stay
    With *Tombs*, then *Cradles*, to weare out a day.
Since such loves naturall lation is, may still
    My love descend, and journey downe the hill,
Not panting after growing beauties, so,
    I shall ebbe out with them, who home-ward goe.   50

x   *The Dreame*

Image of her whom I love, more then she,
    Whose faire impression in my faithfull heart,
Makes mee her Medall, and makes her love mee,
    As Kings do coynes, to which their stamps impart
The value: goe, and take my heart from hence,
    Which now is growne too great and good for me:
Honours oppresse weake spirits, and our sense
    Strong objects dull; the more, the lesse wee see.
When you are gone, and *Reason* gone with you,
    Then *Fantasie* is Queene and Soule, and all;   10
She can present joyes meaner then you do;
    Convenient, and more proportionall.
So, if I dreame I have you, I have you,
    For, all our joyes are but fantasticall.
And so I scape the paine, for paine is true;
    And sleepe which locks up sense, doth lock out all.
After a such fruition I shall wake,
    And, but the waking, nothing shall repent;
And shall to love more thankfull Sonnets make,
    Then if more *honour, teares,* and *paines* were spent.
But dearest heart, and dearer image stay;   21
    Alas, true joyes at best are *dreame* enough;
Though you stay here you passe too fast away:
    For even at first lifes *Taper* is a snuffe.
Fill'd with her love, may I be rather grown
Mad with much *heart*, then *ideott* with none.

Since she must go, and I must mourn, come Night,
Environ me with darkness, whilst I write:
Shadow that hell unto me, which alone
I am to suffer when my Love is gone.
Alas the darkest Magick cannot do it,
Thou and greate Hell to boot are shadows to it.
Should *Cinthia* quit thee, *Venus*, and each starre,
It would not forme one thought dark as mine are.
I could lend thee obscureness now, and say,
Out of my self, There should be no more Day,   10
Such is already my felt want of sight,
Did not the fires within me force a light.
Oh Love, that fire and darkness should be mixt,
Or to thy Triumphs soe strange torments fixt?
Is't because thou thy self art blind, that wee
Thy Martyrs must no more each other see?
Or tak'st thou pride to break us on the wheel,
And view old Chaos in the Pains we feel?
Or have we left undone some mutual Right,
Through holy fear, that merits thy despight?   20
No, no. The falt was mine, impute it to me,
Or rather to conspiring destinie,
Which (since I lov'd for forme before) decreed,
That I should suffer when I lov'd indeed:
And therefore now, sooner then I can say,
I saw the golden fruit, 'tis rapt away.
Or as I had watcht one drop in a vast stream,
And I left wealthy only in a dream.
Yet Love, thou'rt blinder then thy self in this,
To vex my Dove-like friend for my amiss: 30
And, where my own sad truth may expiate
Thy wrath, to make her fortune run my fate:
So blinded Justice doth, when Favorites fall,
Strike them, their house, their friends, their followers all.
Was't not enough that thou didst dart thy fires
Into our blouds, inflaming our desires,
And made'st us sigh and glow, and pant, and burn,
And then thy self into our flame did'st turn?

Was't not enough, that thou didst hazard us
To paths in love so dark, so dangerous: 40
And those so ambush'd round with houshold spies,
And over all, thy husbands towring eyes
That flam'd with oylie sweat of jealousie:
Yet went we not still on with Constancie?
Have we not kept our guards, like spie on spie?
Had correspondence whilst the foe stood by?
Stoln (more to sweeten them) our many blisses
Of meetings, conference, embracements, kisses?
Shadow'd with negligence our most respects?
Varied our language through all dialects,   50
Of becks, winks, looks, and often under-boards
Spoak dialogues with our feet far from our words?
Have we prov'd all these secrets of our Art,
Yea, thy pale inwards, and thy panting heart?
And, after all this passed Purgatory,
Must sad divorce make us the vulgar story?
First let our eyes be rivited quite through
Our turning brains, and both our lips grow to:
Let our armes clasp like Ivy, and our fear
Freese us together, that we may stick here,   60
Till Fortune, that would rive us, with the deed
Strain her eyes open, and it make them bleed:
For Love it cannot be, whom hitherto
I have accus'd, should such a mischief doe.
Oh Fortune, thou'rt not worth my least exclame,
And plague enough thou hast in thy own shame.
Do thy great worst, my friend and I have armes,
Though not against thy strokes, against thy harmes.
Rend us in sunder, thou canst not divide
Our bodies so, but that our souls are ty'd,   70
And we can love by letters still and gifts,
And thoughts and dreams; Love never wanteth shifts.
I will not look upon the quickning Sun,
But straight her beauty to my sense shall run;
The ayre shall note her soft, the fire most pure;
Water suggest her clear, and the earth sure.
Time shall not lose our passages; the Spring
How fresh our love was in the beginning;

The Summer how it ripened in the eare;
And Autumn, what our golden harvests were.   80
The Winter I'll not think on to spite thee,
But count it a lost season, so shall shee.
And dearest Friend, since we must part, drown night
With hope of Day, burthens well born are light.
Though cold and darkness longer hang somewhere,
Yet *Phoebus* equally lights all the Sphere.
And what he cannot in like Portions pay,
The world enjoyes in Mass, and so we may.
Be then ever your self, and let no woe
Win on your health, your youth, your beauty: so   90
Declare your self base fortunes Enemy,
No less by your contempt then constancy:
That I may grow enamoured on your mind,
When my own thoughts I there reflected find.
For this to th'comfort of my Dear I vow,
My Deeds shall still be what my words are now;
The Poles shall move to teach me ere I start;
And when I change my Love, I'll change my heart;
Nay, if I wax but cold in my desire,
Think, heaven hath motion lost, and the world, fire: 100
Much more I could, but many words have made
That, oft, suspected which men would perswade;
Take therefore all in this: I love so true,
As I will never look for less in you.

xvi   *On his Mistris*

By our first strange and fatall interview,
By all desires which thereof did ensue,
By our long starving hopes, by that remorse
Which my words masculine perswasive force
Begot in thee, and by the memory
Of hurts, which spies and rivals threatned me,
I calmly beg: But by thy fathers wrath,
By all paines, which want and divorcement hath,
I conjure thee, and all the oathes which I
And thou have sworne to seale joynt constancy,   10

Here I unsweare, and overswear them thus,
Thou shalt not love by wayes so dangerous.
Temper, ô faire Love, loves impetuous rage,
Be my true Mistris still, not my faign'd Page;
I'll goe, and, by thy kinde leave, leave behinde
Thee, onely worthy to nurse in my minde,
Thirst to come backe; ô if thou die before,
My soule from other lands to thee shall soare.
Thy (else Almighty) beautie cannot move
Rage from the Seas, nor thy love teach them love,   20
Nor tame wilde Boreas harshnesse; Thou hast reade
How roughly hee in peeces shivered
Faire Orithea, whom he swore he lov'd.
Fall ill or good, 'tis madnesse to have prov'd
Dangers unurg'd; Feed on this flattery,
That absent Lovers one in th'other be.
Dissemble nothing, not a boy, nor change
Thy bodies habite, nor mindes; bee not strange
To thy selfe onely; All will spie in thy face
A blushing womanly discovering grace;   30
Richly cloath'd Apes, are call'd Apes, and as soone
Ecclips'd as bright we call the Moone the Moone.
Men of France, changeable Camelions,
Spittles of diseases, shops of fashions,
Loves fuellers, and the rightest company
Of Players, which upon the worlds stage be,
Will quickly know thee, and know thee, and alas
Th'indifferent Italian, as we passe
His warme land, well content to thinke thee Page,
Will hunt thee with such lust, and hideous rage,   40
As *Lots* faire guests were vext. But none of these
Nor spungy hydroptique Dutch shall thee displease,
If thou stay here. O stay here, for, for thee
England is onely a worthy Gallerie,
To walke in expectation, till from thence
Our greatest King call thee to his presence.
When I am gone, dreame me some happinesse,
Nor let thy lookes our long hid love confesse,
Nor praise, nor dispraise me, nor blesse nor curse
Openly loves force, nor in bed fright thy Nurse   50

With midnights startings, crying out, oh, oh
Nurse, ô my love is slaine, I saw him goe
O'r the white Alpes alone; I saw him I,
Assail'd, fight, taken, stabb'd, bleed, fall, and die.
Augure me better chance, except dread *Jove*
Thinke it enough for me to'have had thy love.

xviii   *Loves Progress*

Who ever loves, if he do not propose
The right true end of love, he's one that goes
To sea for nothing but to make him sick:
Love is a bear-whelp born, if we o're lick
Our love, and force it new strange shapes to take,
We erre, and of a lump a monster make.
Were not a Calf a monster that were grown
Face'd like a man, though better then his own?
Perfection is in unitie: preferr
One woman first, and then one thing in her.   10
I, when I value gold, may think upon
The ductilness, the application,
The wholsomness, the ingenuitie,
From rust, from soil, from fire ever free:
But if I love it, 'tis because 'tis made
By our new nature (Use) the soul of trade.
   All these in women we might think upon
(If women had them) and yet love but one.
Can men more injure women then to say
They love them for that, by which they're not they?   20
Makes virtue woman? must I cool my bloud
Till I both be, and find one wise and good?
May barren Angels love so. But if we
Make love to woman; virtue is not she:
As beauty'is not nor wealth: He that strayes thus
From her to hers, is more adulterous,
Then if he took her maid. Search every spheare
And firmament, our *Cupid* is not there:
He's an infernal god and under ground,
With *Pluto* dwells, where gold and fire abound: 30

Men to such Gods, their sacrificing Coles
Did not in Altars lay, but pits and holes.
Although we see Celestial bodies move
Above the earth, the earth we Till and love:
So we her ayres contemplate, words and heart,
And virtues; but we love the Centrique part.
   Nor is the soul more worthy, or more fit
For love, then this, as infinite as it.
But in attaining this desired place
How much they erre; that set out at the face?   40
The hair a Forest is of Ambushes,
Of springes, snares, fetters and manacles:
The brow becalms us when 'tis smooth and plain,
And when 'tis wrinckled, shipwracks us again.
Smooth, 'tis a Paradice, where we would have
Immortal stay, and wrinkled 'tis our grave.
The Nose (like to the first Meridian) runs
Not 'twixt an East and West, but 'twixt two suns;
It leaves a Cheek, a rosie Hemisphere
On either side, and then directs us where   50
Upon the Islands fortunate we fall,
(Not faynte *Canaries,* but *Ambrosiall*)
Her swelling lips; To which when wee are come,
We anchor there, and think our selves at home,
For they seem all: there Syrens songs, and there
Wise Delphick Oracles do fill the ear;
There in a Creek where chosen pearls do swell,
The Remora, her cleaving tongue doth dwell.
These, and the glorious Promontory, her Chin
Ore past; and the streight *Hellespont* betweene   60
The *Sestos* and *Abydos* of her breasts,
(Not of two Lovers, but two Loves the neasts)
Succeeds a boundless sea, but yet thine eye
Some Island moles may scattered there descry;
And Sailing towards her *India,* in that way
Shall at her fair Atlantick Navell stay;
Though thence the Current be thy Pilot made,
Yet ere thou be where thou wouldst be embay'd,
Thou shalt upon another Forest set,
Where many Shipwrack, and no further get.   70

When thou art there, consider what this chace
Mispent by thy beginning at the face.
    Rather set out below; practice my Art,
Some Symetry the foot hath with that part
Which thou dost seek, and is thy Map for that
Lovely enough to stop, but not stay at:
Least subject to disguise and change it is;
Men say the Devil never can change his.
It is the Emblem that hath figured
Firmness; 'tis the first part that comes to bed.   80
Civilitie we see refin'd: the kiss
Which at the face began, transplanted is,
Since to the hand, since to the Imperial knee,
Now at the Papal foot delights to be:
If Kings think that the nearer way, and do
Rise from the foot, Lovers may do so too;
For as free Spheres move faster far then can
Birds, whom the air resists, so may that man
Which goes this empty and Ætherial way,
Then if at beauties elements he stay.   90
Rich Nature hath in women wisely made
Two purses, and their mouths aversely laid:
They then, which to the lower tribute owe,
That way which that Exchequer looks, must go:
He which doth not, his error is as great,
As who by Clyster gave the Stomack meat.

xix   Going to Bed

Come, Madam, come, all rest my powers defie,
Until I labour, I in labour lie.
The foe oft-times having the foe in sight,
Is tir'd with standing though he never fight.
Off with that girdle, like heavens Zone glittering,
But a far fairer world incompassing.
Unpin that spangled breastplate which you wear,
That th'eyes of busie fooles may be stopt there.
Unlace your self, for that harmonious chyme,
Tells me from you, that now it is bed time.   10

Off with that happy busk, which I envie,
That still can be, and still can stand so nigh.
Your gown going off, such beautious state reveals,
As when from flowry meads th'hills shadow steales.
Off with that wyerie Coronet and shew
The haiery Diademe which on you doth grow:
Now off with those shooes, and then safely tread
In this loves hallow'd temple, this soft bed.
In such white robes, heaven's Angels us'd to be
Receavd by men; Thou Angel bringst with thee   20
A heaven like Mahomets Paradise; and though
Ill spirits walk in white, we easly know,
By this these Angels from an evil sprite,
Those set our hairs, but these our flesh upright.

    Licence my roaving hands, and let them go,
Before, behind, between, above, below.
O my America! my new-found-land,
My kingdome, safeliest when with one man man'd,
My Myne of precious stones, My Emperie,
How blest am I in this discovering thee!   30
To enter in these bonds, is to be free;
Then where my hand is set, my seal shall be.

    Full nakedness! All joyes are due to thee,
As souls unbodied, bodies uncloth'd must be,
To taste whole joyes. Gems which you women use
Are like Atlanta's balls, cast in mens views,
That when a fools eye lighteth on a Gem,
His earthly soul may covet theirs, not them.
Like pictures, or like books gay coverings made
For lay-men, are all women thus array'd;   40
Themselves are mystick books, which only wee
(Whom their imputed grace will dignifie)
Must see reveal'd. Then since that I may know;
As liberally, as to a Midwife, shew
Thy self: cast all, yea, this white lynnen hence,
There is no pennance due to innocence.

    To teach thee, I am naked first; why then
What needst thou have more covering than a man.

Epithalamion made at Lincolnes Inne

The Sun-beames in the East are spred,
Leave, leave, faire Bride, your solitary bed,
   No more shall you returne to it alone,
It nourseth sadnesse, and your bodies print,
Like to a grave, the yielding downe doth dint;
     You and your other you meet there anon;
     Put forth, put forth that warme balme-breathing thigh,
Which when next time you in these sheets wil smother,
    There it must meet another,
        Which never was, but must be, oft, more nigh;   10
Come glad from thence, goe gladder then you came,
To day put on perfection, and a womans name.

Daughters of London, you which bee
Our Golden Mines, and furnish'd Treasurie,
   You which are Angels, yet still bring with you
Thousands of Angels on your mariage daies,
Help with your presence and devise to praise
     These rites, which also unto you grow due;
     Conceitedly dresse her, and be assign'd,
By you, fit place for every flower and jewell,   20
    Make her for love fit fewell
        As gay as Flora, and as rich as Inde;
So may shee faire, rich, glad, and in nothing lame,
To day put on perfection, and a womans name.

And you frolique Patricians,
Sonnes of these Senators, wealths deep oceans,
   Ye painted courtiers, barrels of others wits,
Yee country men, who but your beasts love none,
Yee of those fellowships whereof hee's one,
     Of study and play made strange Hermaphrodits,   30
    Here shine; This Bridegroom to the Temple bring.
Loe, in yon path which store of straw'd flowers graceth,
    The sober virgin paceth;

    [*Epithalamion made at Lincolnes Inne*] 90

Except my sight faile, 'tis no other thing;
Weep not nor blush, here is no griefe nor shame,
To day put on perfection, and a womans name.

Thy two-leav'd gates faire Temple unfold,
And these two in thy sacred bosome hold,
  Till, mystically joyn'd, but one they bee;
Then may thy leane and hunger-starved wombe   40
Long time expect their bodies and their tombe,
  Long after their owne parents fatten thee.
  All elder claimes, and all cold barrennesse,
All yeelding to new loves bee far for ever,
    Which might these two dissever,
      All wayes all th'other may each one possesse;
For, the best Bride, best worthy of praise and fame,
To day puts on perfection, and a womans name.

Oh winter dayes bring much delight,
Not for themselves, but for they soon bring night;   50
  Other sweets wait thee then these diverse meats,
Other disports then dancing jollities,
Other love tricks then glancing with the eyes,
  But that the Sun still in our halfe Spheare sweates;
  Hee flies in winter, but he now stands still.
Yet shadowes turne; Noone point he hath attain'd,
  His steeds nill bee restrain'd,
    But gallop lively downe the Westerne hill;
Thou shalt, when he hath runne the worlds half frame,
To night put on perfection, and a womans name.   60

The amorous evening starre is rose,
Why then should not our amorous starre inclose
  Her selfe in her wish'd bed? Release your strings
Musicians, and dancers take some truce
With these your pleasing labours, for great use
  As much wearinesse as perfection brings;
  You and not only you, but all toyl'd beasts
Rest duly; at night all their toyles are dispensed;
  But in their beds commenced
    Are other labours, and more dainty feasts;   70

She goes a maid, who, least she turne the same,
To night puts on perfection, and a womans name.

Thy virgins girdle now untie,
And in thy nuptiall bed (loves altar) lye
   A pleasing sacrifice; now dispossesse
Thee of these chaines and robes which were put on
T'adorne the day, not thee; for thou, alone,
   Like vertue'and truth, art best in nakednesse;
    This bed is onely to virginitie
A grave, but, to a better state, a cradle;   80
    Till now thou wast but able
        To be what now thou art; then that by thee
No more be said, *I may bee,* but, *I am,*
To night put on perfection, and a womans name.

Even like a faithfull man content,
That this life for a better should be spent,
   So, shee a mothers rich stile doth preferre,
And at the Bridegroomes wish'd approach doth lye,
Like an appointed lambe, when tenderly
   The priest comes on his knees t'embowell her;   90
   Now sleep or watch with more joy; and O light
Of heaven, to morrow rise thou hot, and early;
    This Sun will love so dearely
        Her rest, that long, long we shall want her sight;
Wonders are wrought, for shee which had no maime,
To night puts on perfection, and a woman's name.

iii *"Kinde pitty chokes my spleene"*

Kinde pitty chokes my spleene; brave scorn forbids
Those teares to issue which swell my eye-lids;
I must not laugh, nor weepe sinnes, and be wise,
Can railing then cure these worne maladies?
Is not our Mistresse faire Religion,
As worthy of all our Soules devotion,
As vertue was to the first blinded age?
Are not heavens joyes as valiant to asswage
Lusts, as earths honour was to them? Alas,
As wee do them in meanes, shall they surpasse   10
Us in the end, and shall thy fathers spirit
Meete blinde Philosophers in heaven, whose merit
Of strict life may be imputed faith, and heare
Thee, whom hee taught so easie wayes and neare
To follow, damn'd? O if thou dar'st feare this;
This feare great courage, and high valour is.
Dar'st thou ayd mutinous Dutch, and dar'st thou lay
Thee in ships woodden Sepulchers, a prey
To leaders rage, to stormes, to shot, to dearth?
Dar'st thou dive seas, and dungeons of the earth?   20
Hast thou couragious fire to thaw the ice
Of frozen North discoveries? and thrise
Colder than Salamanders, like divine
Children in th'oven, fires of Spaine, and the line,
Whose countries limbecks to our bodies bee,
Canst thou for gaine beare? and must every hee
Which cryes not, Goddesse, to thy Mistresse, draw,
Or eate thy poysonous words? courage of straw!
O desperate coward, wilt thou seeme bold, and
To thy foes and his (who made thee to stand   30
Sentinell in his worlds garrison) thus yeeld,
And for forbidden warres, leave th'appointed field?
Know thy foes: The foule Devill (whom thou
Strivest to please,) for hate, not love, would allow
Thee faine, his whole Realme to be quit; and as

The worlds all parts wither away and passe,
So the worlds selfe, thy other lov'd foe, is
In her decrepit wayne, and thou loving this,
Dost love a withered and worne strumpet; last,   39
Flesh (it selfes death) and joyes which flesh can taste,
Thou lovest; and thy faire goodly soule, which doth
Give this flesh power to taste joy, thou dost loath.
Seeke true religion. O where? Mirreus
Thinking her unhous'd here, and fled from us,
Seekes her at Rome, there, because hee doth know
That shee was there a thousand yeares agoe,
He loves her ragges so, as wee here obey
The statecloth where the Prince sate yesterday.
Crantz to such brave Loves will not be inthrall'd,
But loves her onely, who at Geneva is call'd   50
Religion, plaine, simple, sullen, yong,
Contemptuous, yet unhansome; As among
Lecherous humors, there is one that judges
No wenches wholsome, but course country drudges.
Graius stayes still at home here, and because
Some Preachers, vile ambitious bauds, and lawes
Still new like fashions, bid him thinke that shee
Which dwels with us, is onely perfect, hee
Imbraceth her, whom his Godfathers will
Tender to him, being tender, as Wards still   60
Take such wives as their Guardians offer, or
Pay valewes. Carelesse Phrygius doth abhorre
All, because all cannot be good, as one
Knowing some women whores, dares marry none.
Graccus loves all as one, and thinkes that so
As women do in divers countries goe
In divers habits, yet are still one kinde,
So doth, so is Religion; and this blind-
nesse too much light breeds; but unmoved thou
Of force must one, and forc'd but one allow;   70
And the right; aske thy father which is shee,
Let him aske his; though truth and falshood bee
Neare twins, yet truth a little elder is;
Be busie to seeke her, beleeve mee this,
Hee's not of none, nor worst, that seekes the best.

[III "Kinde pitty chokes my spleene"]   94

To adore, or scorne an image, or protest,
May all be bad; doubt wisely; in strange way
To stand inquiring right, is not to stray;
To sleepe, or runne wrong, is. On a huge hill,
Cragged, and steep, Truth stands, and hee that will   80
Reach her, about must, and about must goe;
And what the hills suddennes resists, winne so;
Yet strive so, that before age, deaths twilight,
Thy Soule rest, for none can worke in that night.
To will, implyes delay, therefore now doe:
Hard deeds, the bodies paines; hard knowledge too
The mindes indeavours reach, and mysteries
Are like the Sunne, dazling, yet plaine to all eyes.
Keepe the truth which thou hast found; men do not stand
In so ill case here, that God hath with his hand   90
Sign'd Kings blanck-charters to kill whom they hate,
Nor are they Vicars, but hangmen to Fate.
Foole and wretch, wilt thou let thy Soule be tyed
To mans lawes, by which she shall not be tryed
At the last day? Oh, will it then boot thee
To say a Philip, or a Gregory,
A Harry, or a Martin taught thee this?
Is not this excuse for mere contraries,
Equally strong? cannot both sides say so?   99
That thou mayest rightly obey power, her bounds know;
Those past, her nature, and name is chang'd; to be
Then humble to her is idolatrie.
As streames are, Power is; those blest flowers that dwell
At the rough streames calme head, thrive and do well,
But having left their roots, and themselves given
To the streames tyrannous rage, alas, are driven
Through mills, and rockes, and woods, and at last, almost
Consum'd in going, in the sea are lost:
So perish Soules, which more chuse mens unjust
Power from God claym'd, then God himselfe to trust.   110

The Storme

TO MR. CHRISTOPHER BROOKE

Thou which art I, ('tis nothing to be soe)
Thou which art still thy selfe, by these shalt know
Part of our passage; And, a hand, or eye
By *Hilliard* drawne, is worth an history,
By a worse painter made; and (without pride)
When by thy judgment they are dignifi'd,
My lines are such: 'Tis the preheminence
Of friendship onely to'impute excellence.
England to whom we'owe, what we be, and have,
Sad that her sonnes did seeke a forraine grave   10
(For, Fates, or Fortunes drifts none can soothsay,
Honour and misery have one face and way.)
From out her pregnant intrailes sigh'd a winde
Which at th'ayres middle marble roome did finde
Such strong resistance, that it selfe it threw
Downeward againe; and so when it did view
How in the port, our fleet deare time did leese,
Withering like prisoners, which lye but for fees,
Mildly it kist our sailes, and, fresh and sweet,
As to a stomack sterv'd, whose insides meete,   20
Meate comes, it came; and swole our sailes, when wee
So joyd, as *Sara*'her swelling joy'd to see.
But 'twas but so kinde, as our countrimen,
Which bring friends one dayes way, and leave them then.
Then like two mighty Kings, which dwelling farre
Asunder, meet against a third to warre,
The South and West winds joyn'd, and, as they blew,
Waves like a rowling trench before them threw.
Sooner then you read this line, did the gale,
Like shot, not fear'd till felt, our sailes assaile;   30
And what at first was call'd a gust, the same
Hath now a stormes, anon a tempests name.
Jonas, I pitty thee, and curse those men,
Who, when the storm rag'd most, did wake thee then;

Sleepe is paines easiest salve, and doth fulfill
All offices of death, except to kill.
But when I wakt, I saw, that I saw not;
I, and the Sunne, which should teach mee'had forgot
East, West, Day, Night, and I could onely say,
If'the world had lasted, now it had beene day.   40
Thousands our noyses were, yet wee'mongst all
Could none by his right name, but thunder call:
Lightning was all our light, and it rain'd more
Then if the Sunne had drunke the sea before.
Some coffin'd in their cabbins lye,'equally
Griev'd that they are not dead, and yet must dye;
And as sin-burd'ned soules from graves will creepe,
At the last day, some forth their cabbins peepe:
And tremblingly'aske what newes, and doe heare so,
Like jealous husbands, what they would not know.   50
Some sitting on the hatches, would seeme there,
With hideous gazing to feare away feare.
Then note they the ships sicknesses, the Mast
Shak'd with this ague, and the Hold and Wast
With a salt dropsie clog'd, and all our tacklings
Snapping, like too-high-stretched treble strings.
And from our totterd sailes, ragges drop downe so,
As from one hang'd in chaines, a yeare agoe.
Even our Ordinance plac'd for our defence,
Strive to breake loose, and scape away from thence.   60
Pumping hath tir'd our men, and what's the gaine?
Seas into seas throwne, we suck in againe;
Hearing hath deaf'd our saylers; and if they
Knew how to heare, there's none knowes what to say.
Compar'd to these stormes, death is but a qualme,
Hell somewhat lightsome, and the'Bermuda calme.
Darknesse, lights elder brother, his birth-right
Claims o'r this world, and to heaven hath chas'd light.
All things are one, and that one none can be,
Since all formes, uniforme deformity   70
Doth cover, so that wee, except God say
Another *Fiat,* shall have no more day.
So violent, yet long these furies bee,
That though thine absence sterve me,'I wish not thee.

The Calme

Our storme is past, and that storms tyrannous rage,
A stupid calme, but nothing it, doth swage.
The fable is inverted, and farre more
A blocke afflicts, now, then a storke before.
Stormes chafe, and soone weare out themselves, or us;
In calmes, Heaven laughs to see us languish thus.
As steady'as I can wish, that my thoughts were,
Smooth as thy mistresse glasse, or what shines there,
The sea is now. And, as the Iles which wee
Seeke, when wee can move, our ships rooted bee.   10
As water did in stormes, now pitch runs out:
As lead, when a fir'd Church becomes one spout.
And all our beauty, and our trimme, decayes,
Like courts removing, or like ended playes.
The fighting place now seamens ragges supply;
And all the tackling is a frippery.
No use of lanthornes; and in one place lay
Feathers and dust, to day and yesterday.
Earths hollownesses, which the worlds lungs are,
Have no more winde then the upper valt of aire.   20
We can nor lost friends, nor sought foes recover,
But meteorlike, save that wee move not, hover.
Onely the Calenture together drawes
Deare friends, which meet dead in great fishes jawes:
And on the hatches as on Altars lyes
Each one, his owne Priest, and owne Sacrifice.
Who live, that miracle do multiply
Where walkers in hot Ovens, doe not dye.
If in despite of these, wee swimme, that hath
No more refreshing, then our brimstone Bath,   30
But from the sea, into the ship we turne,
Like parboyl'd wretches, on the coales to burne.
Like *Bajazet* encag'd, the shepheards scoffe,
Or like slacke sinew'd *Sampson*, his haire off,
Languish our ships. Now, as a Miriade
Of Ants, durst th'Emperours lov'd snake invade,
The crawling Gallies, Sea-gaoles, finny chips,
Might brave our Pinnaces, now bed-ridde ships.

Whether a rotten state, and hope of gaine,
Or to disuse mee from the queasie paine   40
Of being belov'd, and loving, or the thirst
Of honour, or faire death, out pusht mee first,
I lose my end: for here as well as I
A desperate may live, and a coward die.
Stagge, dogge, and all which from, or towards flies,
Is paid with life, or pray, or doing dyes.
Fate grudges us all, and doth subtly lay
A scourge,'gainst which wee all forget to pray,
He that at sea prayes for more winde, as well
Under the poles may begge cold, heat in hell.   50
What are wee then? How little more alas
Is man now, then before he was? he was
Nothing; for us, wee are for nothing fit;
Chance, or our selves still disproportion it.
Wee have no power, no will, no sense; I lye,
I should not then thus feele this miserie.

To Sir Henry Wotton

Sir, more than kisses, letters mingle Soules;
For, thus friends absent speake. This ease controules
The tediousnesse of my life: But for these
I could ideate nothing, which could please,
But I should wither in one day, and passe
To'a bottle'of Hay, that am a locke of Grasse.
Life is a voyage, and in our lifes wayes
Countries, Courts, Towns are Rockes, or Remoraes;
They breake or stop all ships, yet our state's such,
That though then pitch they staine worse, wee must touch.
If in the furnace of the even line,   11
Or under th'adverse icy poles thou pine,
Thou know'st two temperate Regions girded in,
Dwell there: But Oh, what refuge canst thou winne
Parch'd in the Court, and in the country frozen?
Shall cities, built of both extremes, be chosen?
Can dung and garlike be'a perfume? or can
A Scorpion and Torpedo cure a man?

Cities are worst of all three; of all three
(O knottie riddle) each is worst equally.   20
Cities are Sepulchers; they who dwell there
Are carcases, as if no such there were.
And Courts are Theaters, where some men play
Princes, some slaves, all to one end, and of one clay.
The Country is a desert, where no good,
Gain'd (as habits, not borne,) is understood.
There men become beasts, and prone to more evils;
In cities blockes, and in a lewd court, devills.
As in the first Chaos confusedly
Each elements qualities were in the'other three;   30
So pride, lust, covetize, being severall
To these three places, yet all are in all,
And mingled thus, their issue incestuous.
Falshood is denizen'd. Virtue is barbarous.
Let no man say there, Virtues flintie wall
Shall locke vice in mee, I'll do none, but know all.
Men are spunges, which to poure out, receive.
Who know false play, rather then lose, deceive.
For in best understandings, sinne beganne,
Angels sinn'd first, then Devills, and then man.   40
Onely perchance beasts sinne not; wretched wee
Are beasts in all, but white integritie.
I thinke if men, which in these places live
Durst looke for themselves, and themselves retrive,
They would like strangers greet themselves, seeing than
Utopian youth, growne old Italian.
    Be thou thine owne home, and in thy selfe dwell;
Inne any where, continuance maketh hell.
And seeing the snaile, which every where doth rome,
Carrying his owne house still, still is at home,   50
Follow (for he is easie pac'd) this snaile,
Bee thine owne Palace, or the world's thy gaile.
And in the worlds sea, do not like corke sleepe
Upon the waters face; nor in the deepe
Sinke like a lead without a line: but as
Fishes glide, leaving no print where they passe,
Nor making sound; so closely thy course goe,
Let men dispute, whether thou breathe, or no.

Onely'in this one thing, be no Galenist: To make
Courts hot ambitions wholesome, do not take   60
A dramme of Countries dulnesse; do not adde
Correctives, but as chymiques, purge the bad.
But, Sir, I advise not you, I rather doe
Say o'er those lessons, which I learn'd of you:
Whom, free from German schismes, and lightnesse
Of France, and faire Italies faithlesnesse,
Having from these suck'd all they had of worth,
And brought home that faith, which you carried forth,
I throughly love. But if my selfe, I'have wonne
To know my rules, I have, and you have   70
                                        DONNE:

H: W: in Hiber: belligeranti

Went you to conquer? and have so much lost
Yourself, that what in you was best and most,
Respective friendship, should so quickly dye?
In publique gaine my share'is not such that I
Would lose your love for Ireland: better cheap
I pardon death (who though he do not reap
Yet gleanes hee many of our friends away)
Then that your waking mind should bee a prey
To lethargies. Lett shott, and boggs, and skeines
With bodies deale, as fate bids and restreynes;   10
Ere sicknesses attack, yong death is best,
Who payes before his death doth scape arrest.
Lett not your soule (at first with graces fill'd,
And since, and thorough crooked lymbecks, still'd
In many schools and courts, which quicken it,)   15
It self unto the Irish negligence submit.
I aske not labored letters which should weare
Long papers out: nor letters which should feare
Dishonest carriage: or a seers art:
Nor such as from the brayne come, but the hart.   20

To Sir Edward Herbert, at Julyers

Man is a lumpe, where all beasts kneaded bee,
  Wisdome makes him an Arke where all agree;
The foole, in whom these beasts do live at jarre,
  Is sport to others, and a Theater.
Nor scapes hee so, but is himselfe their prey;
  All which was man in him, is eate away,
And now his beasts on one another feed,
  Yet couple'in anger, and new monsters breed.
How happy'is hee, which hath due place assign'd
  To'his beasts, and disaforested his minde!   10
Empail'd himselfe to keepe them out, not in;
  Can sow, and dares trust corne, where they have bin;
Can use his horse, goate, wolfe, and every beast,
  And is not Asse himselfe to all the rest.
Else, man not onely is the heard of swine,
  But he's those devills too, which did incline
Them to a headlong rage, and made them worse:
  For man can adde weight to heavens heaviest curse.
As Soules (they say) by our first touch, take in
  The poysonous tincture of Originall sinne,   20
So, to the punishments which God doth fling,
  Our apprehension contributes the sting.
To us, as to his chickins, he doth cast
  Hemlocke, and wee as men, his hemlocke taste;
We do infuse to what he meant for meat,
  Corrosivenesse, or intense cold or heat.
For, God no such specifique poyson hath
  As kills we know not how; his fiercest wrath
Hath no antipathy, but may be good
  At least for physicke, if not for our food.   30
Thus man, that might be'his pleasure, is his rod,
  And is his devill, that might be his God.
Since then our businesse is, to rectifie
  Nature, to what she was, wee'are led awry
By them, who man to us in little show;
  Greater then due, no forme we can bestow
On him; for Man into himselfe can draw
  All; All his faith can swallow,'or reason chaw.

All that is fill'd, and all that which doth fill,
    All the round world, to man is but a pill,   40
In all it workes not, but it is in all
    Poysonous, or purgative, or cordiall,
For, knowledge kindles Calentures in some,
    And is to others icy *Opium*.
As brave as true, is that profession than
    Which you doe use to make; that you know man.
This makes it credible; you have dwelt upon
    All worthy bookes, and now are such an one.
Actions are authors, and of those in you
    Your friends finde every day a mart of new.   50

To Mr. T. W.

Hast thee harsh verse, as fast as thy lame measure
    Will give thee leave, to him, my pain and pleasure.
I have given thee, and yet thou art too weake,
    Feete, and a reasoning soule and tongue to speake.
Plead for me, and so by thine and my labour
    I am thy Creator, thou my Saviour.
Tell him, all questions, which men have defended
    Both of the place and paines of hell, are ended;
And 'tis decreed our hell is but privation
    Of him, at least in this earths habitation: 10
And 'tis where I am, where in every street
    Infections follow, overtake, and meete:
Live I or die, by you my love is sent,
    And you'are my pawnes, or else my Testament.

An Anatomie of the World: The first Anniversary

Wherein, By occasion of the untimely death of Mistris ELIZABETH DRURY, *the frailty and the decay of this whole World is represented.*

The entrie into the worke.

When that rich Soule which to her
    heaven is gone,
Whom all do celebrate, who know they
    have one,
(For who is sure he hath a Soule, unlesse
It see, and judge, and follow worthi-
    nesse,
And by Deedes praise it? hee who doth
    not this,
May lodge an In-mate soule, but 'tis not
    his.)
When that Queene ended here her prog-
    resse time,
And, as t'her standing house to heaven
    did climbe,
Where loath to make the Saints attend
    her long,
She's now a part both of the Quire, and
    Song,   10
This World, in that great earthquake
    languished;
For in a common bath of teares it bled,
Which drew the strongest vitall spirits
    out:
But succour'd then with a perplexed
    doubt,
Whether the world did lose, or gaine in
    this,
(Because since now no other way there
    is,

But goodnesse, to see her, whom all
    would see,
All must endeavour to be good as shee,)
This great consumption to a fever turn'd,
And so the world had fits; it joy'd, it
    mourn'd;   20
And, as men thinke, that Agues physick
    are,
And th'Ague being spent, give over care,
So thou sicke World, mistak'st thy selfe
    to bee
Well, when alas, thou'rt in a Lethargie.
Her death did wound and tame thee
    than, and than
Thou might'st have better spar'd the
    Sunne, or Man.
That wound was deep, but 'tis more
    misery,
That thou hast lost thy sense and mem-
    ory.
'Twas heavy then to heare thy voyce of
    mone,
But this is worse, that thou art speech-
    lesse growne.   30
Thou hast forgot thy name, thou hadst;
    thou wast
Nothing but shee, and her thou hast
    o'rpast.
For as a child kept from the Font, untill
A prince, expected long, come to fulfill
The ceremonies, thou unnam'd had'st
    laid,
Had not her comming, thee her Palace
    made:
Her name defin'd thee, gave thee forme,
    and frame,
And thou forgett'st to celebrate thy
    name.
Some moneths she hath beene dead (but
    being dead,

Measures of times are all determined)
But long she'ath beene away, long, long,
    yet none   41
Offers to tell us who it is that's gone.
But as in states doubtfull of future
    heires,
When sicknesse without remedie em-
    paires
The present Prince, they're loth it should
    be said,
The Prince doth languish, or the Prince
    is dead:
So mankinde feeling now a generall
    thaw,
A strong example gone, equall to law,
The Cyment which did faithfully com-
    pact,
And glue all vertues, now resolv'd, and
    slack'd,   50
Thought it some blasphemy to say sh'was
    dead,
Or that our weaknesse was discovered
In that confession; therefore spoke no
    more
Then tongues, the Soule being gone, the
    losse deplore.
But though it be too late to succour thee,
Sicke World, yea, dead, yea putrified,
    since shee
Thy'intrinsique balme, and thy preserva-
    tive,
Can never be renew'd, thou never live,
I (since no man can make thee live) will
    try,
What wee may gaine by thy Anatomy.
Her death hath taught us dearely, that
    thou art   61
Corrupt and mortall in thy purest part.
Let no man say, the world it selfe being
    dead,

'Tis labour lost to have discovered
The worlds infirmities, since there is
    none
Alive to study this dissection;

What life the
world hath stil.

For there's a kinde of World remaining
    still,
Though shee which did inanimate and
    fill
The world, be gone, yet in this last long
    night,
Her Ghost doth walke; that is, a glim-
    mering light,   70
A faint weake love of vertue, and of
    good,
Reflects from her, on them which under-
    stood
Her worth; and though she have shut in
    all day,
The twilight of her memory doth stay;
Which, from the carcasse of the old
    world, free,
Creates a new world, and new creatures
    bee
Produc'd: the matter and the stuffe of
    this,
Her vertue, and the forme our practice
    is:
And though to be thus elemented, arme
These creatures, from home-borne in-
    trinsique harme,   80
(For all assum'd unto this dignitie,
So many weedlesse Paradises bee,
Which of themselves produce no venem-
    ous sinne,
Except some forraine Serpent bring it in)
Yet, because outward stormes the
    strongest breake,
And strength it selfe by confidence
    growes weake,
This new world may be safer, being told

The dangers and diseases of the old:
For with due temper men doe then for-
  goe,
Or covet things, when they their true
  worth know.   90

There is no health; Physitians say that
  wee,
At best, enjoy but a neutralitie.
And can there bee worse sicknesse, then
  to know
That we are never well, nor can be so?
Wee are borne ruinous: poore mothers
  cry,
That children come not right, nor or-
  derly;
Except they headlong come and fall
  upon
An ominous precipitation.
How witty's ruine! how importunate
Upon mankinde! it labour'd to frustrate
Even Gods purpose; and made woman,
  sent   101
For mans reliefe, cause of his languish-
  ment.
They were to good ends, and they are so
  still,
But accessory, and principall in ill;
For that first marriage was our funerall:
One woman at one blow, then kill'd us
  all,
And singly, one by one, they kill us now.
We doe delightfully our selves allow
To that consumption; and profusely
  blinde,
Wee kill our selves to propagate our
  kinde.   110
And yet we do not that; we are not men:
There is not now that mankinde, which
  was then,

When as the Sunne and man did seeme
    to strive,

(Joynt tenants of the world) who should
    survive;
When, Stagge, and Raven, and the long-
    liv'd tree,
Compar'd with man, dy'd in minoritie;
When, if a slow pac'd starre had stolne
    away
From the observers marking, he might
    stay
Two or three hundred yeares to see't
    againe,
And then make up his observation
    plaine;   120
When, as the age was long, the sise was
    great;
Mans growth confess'd, and recompenc'd
    the meat;
So spacious and large, that every Soule
Did a faire Kingdome, and large Realme
    controule:
And when the very stature, thus erect,
Did that soule a good way towards
    heaven direct.
Where is this mankinde now? who lives
    to age,
Fit to be made *Methusalem* his page?
Alas, we scarce live long enough to try
Whether a true made clocke run right, or
    lie.   130
Old Grandsires talke of yesterday with
    sorrow,
And for our children wee reserve to mor-
    row.
So short is life, that every peasant
    strives,
In a torne house, or field, to have three
    lives.

[*The first Anniversary*]   109

And as in lasting, so in length is man

Contracted to an inch, who was a
    spanne;
For had a man at first in forrests stray'd,
Or shipwrack'd in the Sea, one would
    have laid
A wager, that an Elephant, or Whale,
That met him, would not hastily assaile
A thing so equall to him: now alas, 141
The Fairies, and the Pigmies well may
    passe
As credible; mankinde decayes so soone,
We'are scarce our Fathers shadowes cast
    at noone:
Onely death addes t'our length: nor are
    wee growne
In stature to be men, till we are none.
But this were light, did our lesse volume
    hold
All the old Text; or had wee chang'd to
    gold
Their silver; or dispos'd into lesse glasse
Spirits of vertue, which then scatter'd
    was.   150
But 'tis not so: w'are not retir'd, but
    dampt;
And as our bodies, so our mindes are
    crampt:
'Tis shrinking, not close weaving that
    hath thus,
In minde, and body both bedwarfed us.
Wee seeme ambitious, Gods whole worke
    t'undoe;
Of nothing hee made us, and we strive
    too,
To bring our selves to nothing backe;
    and wee
Doe what wee can, to do't so soone as
    hee.

With new diseases on our selves we
    warre,
And with new Physicke, a worse Engin
    farre.   160
Thus man, this worlds Vice-Emperour,
    in whom
All faculties, all graces are at home;
And if in other creatures they appeare,
They're but mans Ministers, and Legats
    there,
To worke on their rebellions, and reduce
Them to Civility, and to mans use:
This man, whom God did wooe, and
    loth t'attend
Till man came up, did downe to man
    descend,
This man, so great, that all that is, is
    his,
Oh what a trifle, and poore thing he is!
If man were any thing, he's nothing
    now: 171
Helpe, or at least some time to wast, al-
    low
T'his other wants, yet when he did depart
With her whom we lament, hee lost his
    heart.
She, of whom th'Ancients seem'd to
    prophesie,
When they call'd vertues by the name of
    shee;
Shee in whom vertue was so much re-
    fin'd,
That for Allay unto so pure a minde
Shee tooke the weaker Sex; shee that
    could drive
The poysonous tincture, and the staine
    of *Eve,*   180
Out of her thoughts, and deeds; and
    purifie

All, by a true religious Alchymie;

Shee, shee is dead; shee's dead: when
    thou knowest this,

Thou knowest how poore a trifling thing
    man is.

And learn'st thus much by our Anatomie,

The heart being perish'd, no part can be
    free.

And that except thou feed (not banquet)
    on

The supernaturall food, Religion,

Thy better Growth growes withered, and
    scant;

Be more then man, or thou'rt lesse than
    an Ant.   190

Then, as mankinde, so is the worlds
    whole frame

Quite out of joynt, almost created lame:

For, before God had made up all the
    rest,

Corruption entred, and deprav'd the
    best:

It seis'd the Angels, and then first of all

The world did in her cradle take a fall,

And turn'd her braines, and tooke a
    generall maime,

Wronging each joynt of th'universall
    frame.

The noblest part, man, felt it first; and
    than

Decay of nature Both beasts and plants, curst in the curse
in other parts.   of man.   200

So did the world from the first houre
    decay,

That evening was beginning of the day,

And now the Springs and Sommers
    which we see,

Like sonnes of women after fiftie bee.

And new Philosophy calls all in doubt,

The Element of fire is quite put out;

The Sun is lost, and th'earth, and no
    mans wit
Can well direct him where to looke for it.
And freely men confesse that this world's
    spent,
When in the Planets, and the Firmament
They seeke so many new; they see that
    this   211
Is crumbled out againe to his Atomies.
'Tis all in peeces, all cohaerence gone;
All just supply, and all Relation:
Prince, Subject, Father, Sonne, are
    things forgot,
For every man alone thinkes he hath got
To be a Phoenix and that then can bee
None of that kinde, of which he is, but
    hee.
This is the worlds condition now, and
    now   219
She that should all parts to reunion bow,
She that had all Magnetique force alone,
To draw, and fasten sundred parts in
    one;
She whom wise nature had invented
    then
When she observ'd that every sort of men
Did in their voyage in this worlds Sea
    stray,
And needed a new compasse for their
    way;
She that was best, and first originall
Of all faire copies, and the generall
Steward to Fate; she whose rich eyes,
    and brest
Guilt the West Indies, and perfum'd the
    East;   230
Whose having breath'd in this world,
    did bestow
Spice on those Iles, and bad them still
    smell so,

And that rich Indie which doth gold in-
        terre,
Is but as single money, coyn'd from her:
She to whom this world must it selfe
        refer,
As Suburbs, or the Microcosme of her,
Shee, shee is dead; shee's dead: when
        thou knowst this,
Thou knowst how lame a cripple this
        world is.
And learn'st thus much by our Anatomy,
That this worlds generall sickenesse doth
        not lie   240
In any humour, or one certaine part;
But as thou sawest it rotten at the heart,
Thou seest a Hectique feaver hath got
        hold
Of the whole substance, not to be con-
        trould,
And that thou hast but one way, not
        t'admit
The worlds infection, to be none of it.
For the worlds subtilst immateriall parts
Feele this consuming wound, and ages
        darts.
For the worlds beauty is decai'd, or gone,

Disformity of parts.

Beauty, that's colour, and proportion.
We thinke the heavens enjoy their Spher-
        icall,   251
Their round proportion embracing all.
But yet their various and perplexed
        course,
Observ'd in divers ages, doth enforce
Men to finde out so many Eccentrique
        parts,
Such divers downe-right lines, such over-
        thwarts,
As disproportion that pure forme: It
        teares

The Firmament in eight and forty
  sheires,
And in these Constellations then arise
New starres, and old doe vanish from
  our eyes: 260
As though heav'n suffered earthquakes,
  peace or war,
When new Towers rise, and old demol-
  ish't are.
They have impal'd within a Zodiake
The free-borne Sun, and keepe twelve
  Signes awake
To watch his steps; the Goat and Crab
  controule,
And fright him backe, who else to either
  Pole
(Did not these Tropiques fetter him)
  might runne:
For his course is not round; nor can the
  Sunne
Perfit a Circle, or maintaine his way
One inch direct; but where he rose to-day
He comes no more, but with a couzening
  line,   271
Steales by that point, and so is Serpen-
  tine:
And seeming weary with his reeling
  thus,
He meanes to sleepe, being now falne
  nearer us.
So, of the Starres which boast that they
  doe runne
In Circle still, none ends where he
  begun.
All their proportion's lame, it sinkes, it
  swels.
For of Meridians, and Parallels,
Man hath weav'd out a net, and this net
  throwne

Upon the Heavens, and now they are his
    owne.   280
Loth to goe up the hill, or labour thus
To goe to heaven, we make heaven come
    to us.
We spur, we reine the starres, and in
    their race
They're diversly content t'obey our pace.
But keepes the earth her round propor-
    tion still?
Doth not a Tenarif, or higher Hill
Rise so high like a Rocke, that one might
    thinke
The floating Moone would shipwracke
    there, and sinke?
Seas are so deepe, that Whales being
    strooke to day,
Perchance to morrow, scarce at middle
    way   290
Of their wish'd journies end, the bot-
    tome, die.
And men, to sound depths, so much line
    untie,
As one might justly thinke, that there
    would rise
At end thereof, one of th'Antipodies:
If under all, a Vault infernall bee,
(Which sure is spacious, except that
    we
Invent another torment, that there must
Millions into a strait hot roome be
    thrust)
Then solidnesse, and roundnesse have
    no place.
Are these but warts, and pock-holes in
    the face   300
Of th'earth? Thinke so: but yet confesse,
    in this
The worlds proportion disfigured is;

That those two legges whereon it doth
    rely,
Reward and punishment are bent awry.
And, Oh, it can no more be questioned,
That beauties best, proportion, is dead,
Since even griefe it selfe, which now
    alone
Is left us, is without proportion.
Shee by whose lines proportion should
    bee
Examin'd, measure of all Symmetree,
Whom had that Ancient seen, who
    thought soules made   311
Of Harmony, he would at next have said
That Harmony was shee, and thence
    infer,
That soules were but Resultances from
    her,
And did from her into our bodies goe,
As to our eyes, the formes from objects
    flow:
Shee, who if those great Doctors truly
    said
That the Arke to mans proportions was
    made,
Had been a type for that, as that might
    be
A type of her in this, that contrary   320
Both Elements, and Passions liv'd at
    peace
In her, who caus'd all Civill war to cease.
Shee, after whom, what forme so'er we
    see,
Is discord, and rude incongruitie;
Shee, shee is dead, shee's dead; when
    thou knowst this
Thou knowst how ugly a monster this
    world is:
And learn'st thus much by our Anatomie,
That here is nothing to enamour thee:

And that, not only faults in inward parts,
Corruptions in our braines, or in our
    hearts,   330
Poysoning the fountaines, whence our
    actions spring,
Endanger us: but that if every thing
Be not done fitly'and in proportion,
To satisfie wise, and good lookers on,
(Since most men be such as most thinke
    they bee)
They're lothsome too, by this Deformitee.
For good, and well, must in our actions
    meete;
Wicked is not much worse than indis-
    creet.
But beauties other second Element,   339
Colour, and lustre now, is as neere spent.
And had the world his just proportion,
Were it a ring still, yet the stone is gone.
As a compassionate Turcoyse which
    doth tell
By looking pale, the wearer is not well,
As gold falls sicke being stung with
    Mercury,
All the worlds parts of such complexion
    bee.
When nature was most busie, the first
    weeke,
Swadling the new borne earth, God
    seem'd to like
That she should sport her selfe some-
    times, and play,
To mingle, and vary colours every day:
And then, as though shee could not
    make inow,   351
Himselfe his various Rainbow did allow.
Sight is the noblest sense of any one,
Yet sight hath only colour to feed on,
And colour is decai'd: summers robe
    growes

Duskie, and like an oft dyed garment
  showes.
Our blushing red, which us'd in cheekes
  to spred,
Is inward sunke, and only our soules are
  red.
Perchance the world might have recov-
  ered,
If she whom we lament had not beene
  dead: 360
But shee, in whom all white, and red,
  and blew
(Beauties ingredients) voluntary grew,
As in an unvext Paradise; from whom
Did all things verdure, and their lustre
  come,
Whose composition was miraculous,
Being all colour, all Diaphanous,
(For Ayre, and Fire but thick grosse
  bodies were,
And liveliest stones but drowsie, and
  pale to her,)
Shee, shee, is dead: she's dead: when
  thou know'st this,
Thou knowst how wan a Ghost this our
  world is: 370
And learn'st thus much by our Anatomie,
That it should more affright, then pleas-
  ure thee.
And that, since all faire colour then did
  sinke,
'Tis now but wicked vanitie, to thinke

*Weaknesse in the
want of corre-
spondence of
heaven and earth.*

To colour vicious deeds with good pretence,
Or with bought colors to illude mens
  sense.
Nor in ought more this worlds decay
  appeares,
Then that her influence the heav'n for-
  beares,

Or that the Elements doe not feele this,
The father, or the mother barren is.
The cloudes conceive not raine, or doe
    not powre,   381
In the due birth time, downe the balmy
    showre;
Th'Ayre doth not motherly sit on the
    earth,
To hatch her seasons, and give all
    things birth;
Spring-times were common cradles, but
    are tombes;
And false-conceptions fill the generall
    wombes;
Th'Ayre showes such Meteors, as none
    can see,
Not only what they meane, but what
    they bee;
Earth such new wormes, as would have
    troubled much
Th'Ægyptian *Mages* to have made more
    such.   390
What Artist now dares boast that he can
    bring
Heaven hither, or constellate any thing,
So as the influence of those starres may
    bee
Imprison'd in an Hearbe, or Charme, or
    Tree,
And doe by touch, all which those stars
    could doe?
The art is lost, and correspondence too.
For heaven gives little, and the earth
    takes lesse,
And man least knowes their trade and
    purposes.
If this commerce twixt heaven and earth
    were not
Embarr'd, and all this traffique quite
    forgot,   400

She, for whose losse we have lamented
    thus,
Would worke more fully, and pow'rfully
    on us:
Since herbes, and roots, by dying lose
    not all,
But they, yea Ashes too, are medicinall,
Death could not quench her vertue so,
    but that
It would be (if not follow'd) wondred at:
And all the world would be one dying
    Swan,
To sing her funerall praise, and vanish
    than.
But as some Serpents poyson hurteth
    not,   409
Except it be from the live Serpent shot,
So doth her vertue need her here, to fit
That unto us; shee working more then it.
But shee, in whom to such maturity
Vertue was growne, past growth, that it
    must die;
She, from whose influence all Impres-
    sions came,
But, by Receivers impotencies, lame,
Who, though she could not transubstan-
    tiate
All states to gold, yet guilded every state,
So that some Princes have some tem-
    perance;
Some Counsellers some purpose to ad-
    vance   420
The common profit; and some people
    have
Some stay, no more than Kings should
    give, to crave;
Some women have some taciturnity,
Some nunneries some graines of chas-
    titie.

She that did thus much, and much more
    could doe,
But that our age was Iron, and rustie
    too,
Shee, shee is dead; shee's dead; when
    thou knowst this,
Thou knowst how drie a Cinder this
    world is.
And learn'st thus much by our Anatomy,
That 'tis in vaine to dew, or mollifie
It with thy teares, or sweat, or blood:
    nothing   431
Is worth our travaile, griefe, or perish-
    ing,
But those rich joyes, which did possesse
    her heart,
Of which she's now partaker, and a
    part.

Conclusion.

But as in cutting up a man that's dead,
The body will not last out, to have read
On every part, and therefore men direct
Their speech to parts, that are of most
    effect;
So the worlds carcasse would not last,
    if I
Were punctuall in this Anatomy;   440
Nor smels it well to hearers, if one tell
Them their disease, who faine would
    think they're well.
Here therefore be the end: And, blessed
    maid,
Of whom is meant what ever hath been
    said,
Or shall be spoken well by any tongue,
Whose name refines course lines, and
    makes prose song,
Accept this tribute, and his first yeares
    rent,
Who till his darke short tapers end be
    spent,

As oft as thy feast sees this widowed
    earth,
Will yearely celebrate thy second birth,
That is, thy death; for though the soule
    of man   451
Be got when man is made, 'tis borne but
    than
When man doth die; our body's as the
    wombe,
And, as a Mid-wife, death directs it
    home.
And you her creatures, whom she workes
    upon,
And have your last, and best concoction
From her example, and her vertue, if you
In reverence to her, do thinke it due,
That no one should her praises thus
    rehearse,
As matter fit for Chronicle, not verse;
Vouchsafe to call to minde that God did
    make   461
A last, and lasting'st peece, a song. He
    spake
To *Moses* to deliver unto all,
That song, because hee knew they would
    let fall
The Law, the Prophets, and the History,
But keepe the song still in their memory:
Such an opinion (in due measure) made
Me this great Office boldly to invade:
Nor could incomprehensiblenesse de-
    terre
Mee, from thus trying to emprison her,
Which when I saw that a strict grave
    could doe,   471
I saw not why verse might not do so too.
Verse hath a middle nature: heaven
    keeps Soules,
The Grave keepes bodies, Verse the
    Fame enroules.

Of the Progresse of the Soule: The second Anniversary

Wherein, By occasion of the Religious death of Mistris ELIZABETH DRURY, *the incommodities of the Soule in this life, and her exaltation in the next, are contemplated.*

The entrance.

Nothing could make me sooner to con-
   fesse
That this world had an everlastingnesse,
Then to consider, that a yeare is runne,
Since both this lower world's, and the
   Sunnes Sunne,
The Lustre, and the vigor of this All,
Did set; 'twere blasphemie to say, did
   fall.
But as a ship which hath strooke saile,
   doth runne
By force of that force which before, it
   wonne:
Or as sometimes in a beheaded man,
Though at those two Red seas, which
   freely ranne,   10
One from the Trunke, another from the
   Head,
His soule be sail'd, to her eternall bed,
His eyes will twinckle, and his tongue
   will roll,
As though he beckned, and cal'd backe
   his soule,
He graspes his hands, and he pulls up
   his feet,
And seemes to reach, and to step forth
   to meet
His soule; when all these motions which
   we saw,
Are but as Ice, which crackles at a
   thaw:

Or as a Lute, which in moist weather, rings
    Her knell alone, by cracking of her strings: 20
So struggles this dead world, now shee is gone;
For there is motion in corruption.
As some daies are at the Creation nam'd,
Before the Sunne, the which fram'd daies, was fram'd,
So after this Sunne's set, some shew appeares,
And orderly vicissitude of yeares.
Yet a new Deluge, and of *Lethe* flood,
Hath drown'd us all, All have forgot all good,
Forgetting her, the maine reserve of all.
Yet in this deluge, grosse and generall,
Thou seest me strive for life; my life shall bee,   31
To be hereafter prais'd, for praysing thee;
Immortall Maid, who though thou would'st refuse
The name of Mother, be unto my Muse
A Father, since her chast Ambition is,
Yearely to bring forth such a child as this.
These Hymnes may worke on future wits, and so
May great Grand children of thy prayses grow.
And so, though not revive, embalme and spice
The world, which else would putrifie with vice.   40
For thus, Man may extend thy progeny,
Untill man doe but vanish, and not die.

These Hymnes thy issue, may encrease
　　so long,
As till Gods great *Venite* change the
　　song.

*A just disestima-
tion of this world.*

Thirst for that time, O my insatiate
　　soule,
And serve thy thirst, with Gods safe-
　　sealing Bowle.
Be thirstie still, and drinke still till thou
　　goe
To th'only Health, to be Hydroptique so.
Forget this rotten world; And unto thee
Let thine owne times as an old storie bee.
Be not concern'd: studie not why, nor
　　when;　　　　　　　　　　　51
Doe not so much as not beleeve a man.
For though to erre, be worst, to try truths
　　forth,
Is far more businesse, then this world
　　is worth.
The world is but a carkasse; thou art fed
By it, but as a worme, that carkasse
　　bred;
And why should'st thou, poore worme,
　　consider more,
When this world will grow better then
　　before,
Then those thy fellow wormes doe thinke
　　upon
That carkasses last resurrection.　　60
Forget this world, and scarce thinke of
　　it so,
As of old clothes, cast off a yeare agoe.
To be thus stupid is Alacritie;
Men thus Lethargique have best Mem-
　　ory.
Look upward; that's towards her, whose
　　happy state
We now lament not, but congratulate.

[*The second Anniversary*]　126

Shee, to whom all this world was but a
stage,
Where all sat harkning how her youth-
full age
Should be emploi'd, because in all shee
did,
Some Figure of the Golden times was
hid.
Who could not lacke, what e'r this
world could give,   71
Because shee was the forme, that made
it live;
Nor could complaine, that this world was
unfit
To be staid in, then when shee was in it;
Shee that first tried indifferent desires
By vertue, and vertue by religious fires,
Shee to whose person Paradise adher'd,
As Courts to Princes, shee whose eyes
ensphear'd
Star-light enough, t'have made the South
controule,
(Had shee beene there) the Star-full
Northerne Pole,   80
Shee, shee is gone; she is gone; when
thou knowest this,
What fragmentary rubbidge this world is
Thou knowest, and that it is not worth
a thought;
He honors it too much that thinkes it
nought.

Contemplation of
our state in our
death-bed.

Thinke then, my soule, that death is but
a Groome,
Which brings a Taper to the outward
roome,
Whence thou spiest first a little glim-
mering light,
And after brings it nearer to thy sight:
For such approaches doth heaven make
in death.

Thinke thy selfe labouring now with
    broken breath, 90
And thinke those broken and soft Notes
    to bee
Division, and thy happyest Harmonie.
Thinke thee laid on thy death-bed, loose
    and slacke;
And thinke that, but unbinding of a
    packe,
To take one precious thing, thy soule
    from thence.
Thinke thy selfe parch'd with fevers vio-
    lence,
Anger thine ague more, by calling it
Thy Physicke; chide the slackness of the
    fit.
Thinke that thou hear'st thy knell, and
    think no more,
But that, as Bels cal'd thee to Church
    before, 100
So this, to the Triumphant Church, calls
    thee.
Thinke Satans Sergeants round about
    thee bee,
And thinke that but for Legacies they
    thrust;
Give one thy Pride, to'another give thy
    Lust:
Give them those sinnes which they gave
    thee before,
And trust th'immaculate blood to wash
    thy score.
Thinke thy friends weeping round, and
    thinke that they
Weepe but because they goe not yet thy
    way.
Thinke that they close thine eyes, and
    thinke in this,
That they confesse much in the world,
    amisse, 110

Who dare not trust a dead mans eye
    with that,
Which they from God, and Angels cover
    not.
Thinke that they shroud thee up, and
    think from thence
They reinvest thee in white innocence.
Thinke that thy body rots, and (if so
    low,
Thy soule exalted so, thy thoughts can
    goe,)
Think thee a Prince, who of themselves
    create
Wormes which insensibly devoure their
    State.
Thinke that they bury thee, and thinke
    that right
Laies thee to sleepe but a Saint Lucies
    night.   120
Thinke these things cheerefully: and if
    thou bee
Drowsie or slacke, remember then that
    shee,
Shee whose Complexion was so even
    made,
That which of her Ingredients should
    invade
The other three, no Feare, no Art could
    guesse:
So far were all remov'd from more or
    lesse.
But as in Mithridate, or just perfumes,
Where all good things being met, no
    one presumes
To governe, or to triumph on the rest,
Only because all were, no part was
    best.   130
And as, though all doe know, that quan-
    tities

Are made of lines, and lines from Points
    arise,
None can these lines or quantities un-
    joynt,
And say this is a line, or this a point,
So though the Elements and Humors
    were
In her, one could not say, this governes
    there.
Whose even constitution might have
    wonne
Any disease to venter on the Sunne,
Rather then her: and make a spirit
    feare,
That hee to disuniting subject were. 140
To whose proportions if we would com-
    pare
Cubes, th'arc unstable; Circles, Angu-
    lar;
She who was such a chaine as Fate em-
    ployes
To bring mankinde all Fortunes it en-
    joyes;
So fast, so even wrought, as one would
    thinke,
No Accident could threaten any linke;
Shee, shee embrac'd a sicknesse, gave it
    meat,
The purest blood, and breath, that e'r it
    eate;
And hath taught us, that though a good
    man hath
Title to heaven, and plead it by his
    Faith,   150
And though he may pretend a conquest,
    since
Heaven was content to suffer violence,
Yea though hee plead a long possession
    too,

(For they're in heaven on earth who
    heavens workes do)
Though hee had right and power and
    place, before,
Yet Death must usher, and unlocke the
    doore.

Incommodities of
the Soule in the
Body.

Thinke further on thy selfe, my Soule,
    and thinke
How thou at first wast made but in a
    sinke;
Thinke that it argued some infirmitie,
That those two soules, which then thou
    foundst in me,   160
Thou fedst upon, and drewst into thee,
    both
My second soule of sense, and first of
    growth.
Thinke but how poore thou wast, how
    obnoxious;
Whom a small lumpe of flesh could
    poyson thus.
This curded milke, this poore unlittered
    whelpe
My body, could, beyond escape or helpe,
Infect thee with Originall sinne, and
    thou
Couldst neither then refuse, nor leave it
    now.
Thinke that no stubborne sullen An-
    chorit,
Which fixt to a pillar, or a grave, doth
    sit   170
Bedded, and bath'd in all his ordures,
    dwels
So fowly as our Soules in their first-
    built Cels.
Thinke in how poore a prison thou didst
    lie
After, enabled but to suck, and crie.

[*The second Anniversary*]   131

Thinke, when'twas growne to most,
    'twas a poore Inne,
A Province pack'd up in two yards of
    skinne,
And that usurp'd or threatned with the
    rage
Of sicknesses, or their true mother,
    Age.
But thinke that Death hath now enfran-
    chis'd thee,

*Her liberty by
death.*

Thou hast thy'expansion now, and lib-
    ertie;   180
Thinke that a rustie Peece, discharg'd,
    is flowne
In peeces, and the bullet is his owne,
And freely flies: This to thy Soule al-
    low,
Thinke thy shell broke, thinke thy Soule
    hatch'd but now.
And think this slow-pac'd soule, which
    late did cleave
To'a body, and went but by the bodies
    leave,
Twenty, perchance, or thirty mile a day,
Dispatches in a minute all the way
Twixt heaven, and earth; she stayes not
    in the ayre,
To looke what Meteors there themselves
    prepare;   190
She carries no desire to know, nor sense,
Whether th'ayres middle region be in-
    tense;
For th'Element of fire, she doth not
    know,
Whether she past by such a place or no;
She baits not at the Moone, nor cares to
    trie
Whether in that new world, men live,
    and die.

[*The second Anniversary*] 132

Venus retards her not, to'enquire, how
    shee
Can, (being one starre) *Hesper,* and
    Vesper bee;
Hee that charm'd *Argus* eyes, sweet
    Mercury,
Workes not on her, who now is growne
    all eye;   200
Who, if she meet the body of the Sunne,
Goes through, not staying till his course
    be runne;
Who findes in *Mars* his Campe no corps
    of Guard;
Nor is by *Jove,* nor by his father barr'd;
But ere she can consider how she went,
At once is at, and through the Firma-
    ment.
And as these starres were but so many
    beads
Strung on one string, speed undistin-
    guish'd leads
Her through those Spheares, as through
    the beads, a string,
Whose quick succession makes it still
    one thing: 210
As doth the pith, which, lest our bodies
    slacke,
Strings fast the little bones of necke, and
    backe;
So by the Soule doth death string
    Heaven and Earth;
For when our Soule enjoyes this her
    third birth,
(Creation gave her one, a second,
    grace,)
Heaven is as neare, and present to her
    face,
As colours are, and objects, in a roome
Where darknesse was before, when Ta-
    pers come.

This must, my Soule, thy long-short
  Progresse bee;
To'advance these thoughts, remember
  then, that shee,   220
Shee, whose faire body no such prison
  was,
But that a Soule might well be pleas'd to
  passe
An age in her; she whose rich beauty
  lent
Mintage to other beauties, for they went
But for so much as they were like to her;
Shee, in whose body (if we dare pre-
  ferre
This low world, to so high a marke as
  shee,)
The Westerne treasure, Easterne
  spicerie,
Europe, and Afrique, and the unknowne
  rest
Were easily found, or what in them was
  best;   230
And when w'have made this large dis-
  coverie
Of all, in her some one part then will
  bee
Twenty such parts, whose plenty and
  riches is
Enough to make twenty such worlds as
  this;
Shee, whom had they knowne who did
  first betroth
The Tutelar Angels, and assign'd one,
  both
To Nations, Cities, and to Companies,
To Functions, Offices, and Dignities,
And to each severall man, to him, and
  him,
They would have given her one for every
  limbe;   240

She, of whose soule, if wee may say,
    'twas Gold,
Her body was th'Electrum, and did
    hold
Many degrees of that; wee understood
Her by her sight; her pure, and eloquent
    blood
Spoke in her cheekes, and so distinctly
    wrought,
That one might almost say, her body
    thought;
Shee, shee, thus richly and largely
    hous'd, is gone:
And chides us slow-pac'd snailes who
    crawle upon
Our prisons prison, earth, nor thinke us
    well,
Longer, then whil'st wee beare our brittle
    shell.   250

Her ignorance in this life and knowledge in the next.

But 'twere but little to have chang'd
    our roome,
If, as we were in this our living Tombe
Oppress'd with ignorance, wee still were
    so.
Poore soule, in this thy flesh what dost
    thou know?
Thou know'st thy selfe so little, as thou
    know'st not,
How thou didst die, nor how thou wast
    begot.
Thou neither know'st, how thou at first
    cam'st in,
Nor how thou took'st the poyson of
    mans sinne.
Nor dost thou, (though thou know'st,
    that thou art so)
By what way thou art made immortall,
    know.   260
Thou art too narrow, wretch, to compre-
    hend

Even thy selfe: yea though thou wouldst
    but bend
To know thy body. Have not all soules
    thought
For many ages, that our body'is wrought
Of Ayre, and Fire, and other Elements?
And now they thinke of new ingredients,
And one Soule thinkes one, and another
    way
Another thinkes, and 'tis an even lay.
Knowst thou but how the stone doth
    enter in
The bladders cave, and never breake the
    skinne?   270
Know'st thou how blood, which to the
    heart doth flow,
Doth from one ventricle to th'other goe?
And for the putrid stuffe, which thou
    dost spit,
Know'st thou how thy lungs have at-
    tracted it?
There are no passages, so that there is
(For ought thou know'st) piercing of
    substances.
And of those many opinions which men
    raise
Of Nailes and Haires, dost thou know
    which to praise?
What hope have wee to know our selves,
    when wee
Know not the least things, which for our
    use be?   280
Wee see in Authors, too stiffe to recant,
A hundred controversies of an Ant;
And yet one watches, starves, freeses,
    and sweats,
To know but Catechismes and Alphabets
Of unconcerning things, matters of fact;
How others on our stage their parts did
    Act;

What *Caesar* did, yea, and what *Cicero*
    said.
Why grasse is greene, or why our blood
    is red,
Are mysteries which none have reach'd
    unto.
In this low forme, poore soule, what
    wilt thou doe?   290
When wilt thou shake off this Pedantery,
Of being taught by sense, and Fantasie?
Thou look'st through spectacles; small
    things seeme great
Below; But up unto the watch-towre get,
And see all things despoyl'd of fallacies:
Thou shalt not peepe through lattices of
    eyes,
Nor heare through Labyrinths of eares,
    nor learne
By circuit, or collections to discerne.
In heaven thou straight know'st all, con-
    cerning it,
And what concernes it not, shalt straight
    forget.   300
There thou (but in no other schoole)
    maist bee
Perchance, as learned, and as full, as
    shee,
Shee who all libraries had throughly
    read
At home in her owne thoughts, and prac-
    tised
So much good as would make as many
    more:
Shee whose example they must all im-
    plore,
Who would or doe, or thinke well, and
    confesse
That all the vertuous Actions they ex-
    presse,
Are but a new, and worse edition

Of her some one thought, or one ac-
tion: 310
She who in th'art of knowing Heaven,
was growne
Here upon earth, to such perfection,
That she hath, ever since to Heaven she
came,
(In a far fairer print,) but read the
same:
Shee, shee not satisfied with all this
waight,
(For so much knowledge, as would over-
fraight
Another, did but ballast her) is gone
As well t'enjoy, as get perfection.
And cals us after her, in that shee tooke,

Of our company
in this life, and
in the next.

(Taking her selfe) our best, and worth-
iest booke.   320
Returne not, my Soule, from this ex-
tasie,
And meditation of what thou shalt bee,
To earthly thoughts, till it to thee ap-
peare,
With whom thy conversation must be
there.
With whom wilt thou converse? what
station
Canst thou choose out, free from infec-
tion,
That will not give thee theirs, nor
drinke in thine?
Shalt thou not finde a spungie slacke
Divine
Drinke and sucke in th'instructions of
Great men,
And for the word of God, vent them
agen?   330
Are there not some Courts (and then,
no things bee

So like as Courts) which, in this let us
    see,

That wits and tongues of Libellers are
    weake,

Because they do more ill, then these can
    speake?

The poyson's gone through all, poysons
    affect

Chiefly the chiefest parts, but some ef-
    fect

In nailes, and haires, yea excrements,
    will show;

So lyes the poyson of sinne in the most
    low.

Up, up, my drowsie Soule, where thy
    new eare

Shall in the Angels songs no discord
    heare;   340

Where thou shalt see the blessed Mother-
    maid

Joy in not being that, which men have
    said.

Where she is exalted more for being
    good,

Then for her interest of Mother-hood.

Up to those Patriarchs, which did longer
    sit

Expecting Christ, then they'have enjoy'd
    him yet.

Up to those Prophets, which now gladly
    see

Their Prophesies growne to be Historie.

Up to th'Apostles, who did bravely runne

All the Suns course, with more light
    then the Sunne.   350

Up to those Martyrs, who did calmly
    bleed

Oyle to th'Apostles Lamps, dew to their
    seed.

Up to those Virgins, who thought, that almost
They made joyntenants with the Holy Ghost,
If they to any should his Temple give.
Up, up, for in that squadron there doth live
She, who hath carried thither new degrees
(As to their number) to their dignities.
Shee, who being to her selfe a State, injoy'd
All royalties which any State employ'd;   360
For shee made warres, and triumph'd; reason still
Did not o'rthrow, but rectifie her will:
And she made peace, for no peace is like this,
That beauty, and chastity together kisse:
She did high justice, for she crucified
Every first motion of rebellious pride:
And she gave pardons, and was liberall,
For, onely her selfe except, she pardon'd all:
Shee coy'nd, in this, that her impressions gave
To all our actions all the worth they have: 370
She gave protections; the thoughts of her brest
Satans rude Officers could ne'r arrest.
As these prerogatives being met in one,
Made her a soveraigne State; religion
Made her a Church; and these two made her all.
She who was all this All, and could not fall
To worse, by company, (for she was still

More Antidote, then all the world was
    ill,)
Shee, shee doth leave it, and by Death,
    survive
All this, in Heaven; whither who doth
    not strive   380
The more, because shees there, he doth
    not know
That accidentall joyes in Heaven doe
    grow.
But pause, my soule; And study, ere thou
    fall

Of essentiall joy
in this life and
in the next.

On accidentall joyes, th'essentiall.
Still before Accessories doe abide
A triall, must the principall be tride.
And what essentiall joy can'st thou ex-
    pect
Here upon earth? what permanent ef-
    fect
Of transitory causes? Dost thou love
Beauty? (And beauty worthy'st is to
    move)   390
Poore cousened cousenor, *that* she, and
    that thou,
Which did begin to love, are neither
    now;
You are both fluid, chang'd since yester-
    day;
Next day repaires, (but ill) last dayes
    decay.
Nor are, (although the river keepe the
    name)
Yesterdaies waters, and to daies the
    same.
So flowes her face, and thine eyes,
    neither now
That Saint, nor Pilgrime, which your lov-
    ing vow
Concern'd, remaines; but whil'st you
    thinke you bee

Constant, you'are hourely in incon-
   stancie.   400
Honour may have pretence unto our
   love,
Because that God did live so long above
Without this Honour, and then lov'd it
   so,
That he at last made Creatures to be-
   stow
Honour on him; not that he needed it,
But that, to his hands, man might grow
   more fit.
But since all Honours from inferiours
   flow,
(For they doe give it; Princes doe but
   shew
Whom they would have so honor'd) and
   that this
On such opinions, and capacities   410
Is built, as rise and fall, to more and
   lesse:
Alas, 'tis but a casuall happinesse.
Hath ever any man to'himselfe assign'd
This or that happinesse to'arrest his
   minde,
But that another man which takes a
   worse,
Thinks him a foole for having tane that
   course?
They who did labour Babels tower
   to'erect,
Might have considered, that for that
   effect,
All this whole solid Earth could not al-
   low
Nor furnish forth materialls enow;   420
And that this Center, to raise such a
   place,

Was farre too little, to have beene the
    Base;
No more affords this world, foundation
To erect true joy, were all the meanes in
    one.
But as the Heathen made them severall
    gods,
Of all Gods Benefits, and all his Rods,
(For as the Wine, and Corne, and
    Onions are
Gods unto them, so Agues bee, and
    Warre)
And as by changing that whole precious
    Gold
To such small Copper coynes, they lost
    the old,   430
And lost their only God, who ever must
Be sought alone, and not in such a
    thrust:
So much mankinde true happinesse mis-
    takes;
No Joy enjoyes that man, that many
    makes.
Then, Soule, to thy first pitch worke up
    againe;
Know that all lines which circles doe
    containe,
For once that they the Center touch, doe
    touch
Twice the circumference; and be thou
    such;
Double on heaven thy thoughts on earth
    emploid;
All will not serve; Only who have en-
    joy'd   440
The sight of God, in fulnesse, can thinke
    it;
For it is both the object, and the wit.
This is essentiall joy, where neither hee

Can suffer diminution, nor wee;
'Tis such a full, and such a filling good,
Had th'Angels once look'd on him, they
    had stood.
To fill the place of one of them, or more,
Shee whom wee celebrate, is gone before.
She, who had Here so much essentiall
    joy,
As no chance could distract, much lesse
    destroy;   450
Who with Gods presence was acquainted
    so,
(Hearing, and speaking to him) as to
    know
His face in any naturall Stone, or Tree,
Better then when in Images they bee:
Who kept by diligent devotion,
Gods Image, in such reparation,
Within her heart, that what decay was
    growne,
Was her first Parents fault, and not her
    owne:
Who being solicited to any act,
Still heard God pleading his safe precon-
    tract;   460
Who by a faithfull confidence, was here
Betroth'd to God, and now is married
    there;
Whose twilights were more cleare, then
    our mid-day;
Who dreamt devoutlier, then most use to
    pray;
Who being here fil'd with grace, yet
    strove to bee,
Both where more grace, and more ca-
    pacitie
At once is given: she to Heaven is gone,
Who made this world in some proportion
A heaven, and here, became unto us all,
Joy, (as our joyes admit) essentiall. 470

But could this low world joyes essentiall
 touch,
Heavens accidentall joyes would passe
 them much.
How poore and lame, must then our
 casuall bee?
If thy Prince will his subjects to call
 thee
My Lord, and this doe swell thee, thou
 art than,
By being greater, growne to bee lesse
 Man.
When no Physitian of redresse can
 speake,
A joyfull casuall violence may breake
A dangerous Apostem in thy breast;
And whil'st thou joyest in this, the dan-
 gerous rest,   480
The bag may rise up, and so strangle
 thee.
What e'r was casual, may ever bee.
What should the nature change? Or
 make the same
Certaine, which was but casuall, when it
 came?
All casuall joy doth loud and plainly say,
Only by comming, that it can away.
Only in Heaven joyes strength is never
 spent;
And accidentall things are permanent.
Joy of a soules arrivall ne'r decaies;
For that soule ever joyes and ever
 staies.   490
Joy that their last great Consummation
Approaches in the resurrection;
When earthly bodies more celestiall
Shall be, then Angels were, for they
 could fall;
This kinde of joy doth every day admit
Degrees of growth, but none of losing it.

In this fresh joy, 'tis no small part, that
    shee,
Shee, in whose goodnesse, he that names
    degree,
Doth injure her; ('Tis losse to be cal'd
    best,
There where the stuffe is not such as the
    rest)   500
Shee, who left such a bodie, as even
    shee
Only in Heaven could learne, how it can
    bee
Made better; for shee rather was two
    soules,
Or like to full on both sides written Rols,
Where eyes might reade upon the out-
    ward skin,
As strong Records for God, as mindes
    within;
Shee, who by making full perfection
    grow,
Peeces a Circle, and still keepes it so,
Long'd for, and longing for it, to heaven
    is gone,
Where shee receives, and gives addi-
    tion.   510
Conclusion. Here in a place, where mis-devotion
    frames
A thousand Prayers to Saints, whose
    very names
The ancient Church knew not, Heaven
    knows not yet:
And where, what lawes of Poetry admit,
Lawes of Religion have at least the
    same,
Immortall Maide, I might invoke thy
    name.
Could any Saint provoke that appetite,
Thou here should'st make me a French
    convertite.

But thou would'st not; nor would'st thou
    be content,
To take this, for my second yeares true
    Rent,   520
Did this Coine beare any other stampe,
    then his,
That gave thee power to doe, me, to say
    this.
Since his will is, that to posteritie,
Thou should'st for life, and death, a pat-
    terne bee,
And that the world should notice have of
    this,
The purpose, and th'Authoritie is his;
Thou art the Proclamation; and I am
The Trumpet, at whose voyce the peo-
    ple came.

La Corona

1. LA CORONA

Deigne at my hands this crown of prayer and praise,
Weav'd in my low devout melancholie,
Thou which of good, hast, yea art treasury,
All changing unchang'd Antient of dayes,
But doe not, with a vile crowne of fraile bayes,
Reward my muses white sincerity,
But what thy thorny crowne gain'd, that give mee,
A crowne of Glory, which doth flower alwayes;
The ends crowne our workes, but thou crown'st our ends,
For, at our end begins our endlesse rest,   10
This first last end, now zealously possest,
With a strong sober thirst, my soule attends.
'Tis time that heart and voice be lifted high,
Salvation to all that will is nigh.

2. ANNUNCIATION

Salvation to all that will is nigh.
That All, which alwayes is All every where,
Which cannot sinne, and yet all sinnes must beare,
Which cannot die, yet cannot chuse but die,
Loe, faithfull Virgin, yeelds himselfe to lye
In prison, in thy wombe; and though he there
Can take no sinne, nor thou give, yet he'will weare
Taken from thence, flesh, which deaths force may trie.
Ere by the spheares time was created, thou
Wast in his minde, who is thy Sonne, and Brother,   10
Whom thou conceiv'st, conceiv'd; yea thou art now
Thy Makers maker, and thy Fathers mother,
Thou'hast light in darke; and shutst in little roome,
Immensity cloysterd in thy deare wombe.

3. NATIVITIE

Immensitie cloysterd in thy deare wombe,
Now leaves his welbelov'd imprisonment,

There he hath made himselfe to his intent
Weake enough, now into our world to come;
But Oh, for thee, for him, hath th'Inne no roome?
Yet lay him in this stall, and from the Orient,
Starres, and wisemen will travell to prevent
Th'effect of *Herods* jealous generall doome.
Seest thou, my Soule, with thy faiths eyes, how he
Which fils all place, yet none holds him, doth lye?   10
Was not his pity towards thee wondrous high,
That would have need to be pittied by thee?
Kisse him, and with him into Egypt goe,
With his kinde mother, who partakes thy woe.

4.   TEMPLE

With his kinde mother who partakes thy woe,
Joseph turne backe; see where your child doth sit,
Blowing, yea blowing out those sparks of wit,
Which himselfe on those Doctors did bestow;
The Word but lately could not speake, and loe
It sodenly speakes wonders, whence comes it,
That all which was, and all which should be writ,
A shallow seeming child, should deeply know?
His Godhead was not soule to his manhood,
Nor had time mellowed him to this ripenesse,   10
But as for one which hath a long taske, 'tis good,
With the Sunne to beginne his businesse,
He in his ages morning thus began
By miracles exceeding power of man.

5.   CRUCYFYING

By miracles exceeding power of man,
Hee faith in some, envie in some begat,
For, what weake spirits admire, ambitious, hate;
In both affections many to him ran,
But Oh! the worst are most, they will and can,
Alas, and do, unto the immaculate,
Whose creature Fate is, now prescribe a Fate,
Measuring selfe-lifes infinity to'a span,
Nay to an inch. Loe, where condemned hee
Beares his owne crosse, with paine, yet by and by   10

When it beares him, he must beare more and die.
Now thou art lifted up, draw mee to thee,
And at thy death giving such liberall dole,
Moyst, with one drop of thy blood, my dry soule.

6.   RESURRECTION

Moyst with one drop of thy blood, my dry soule
Shall (though she now be in extreme degree
Too stony hard, and yet too fleshly,) bee
Freed by that drop, from being starv'd, hard, or foule,
And life, by this death abled, shall controule
Death, whom thy death slue; nor shall to mee
Feare of first or last death, bring miserie,
If in thy little booke my name thou enroule,
Flesh in that long sleep is not putrified,
But made that there, of which, and for which 'twas;   10
Nor can by other meanes be glorified.
May then sinnes sleep, and deaths soone from me passe,
That wak't from both, I againe risen may
Salute the last, and everlasting day.

7.   ASCENTION

Salute the last and everlasting day,
Joy at the uprising of this Sunne, and Sonne,
Yee whose just teares, or tribulation
Have purely washt, or burnt your drossie clay;
Behold the Highest, parting hence away,
Lightens the darke clouds, which hee treads upon,
Nor doth hee by ascending, show alone,
But first hee, and hee first enters the way.
O strong Ramme, which hast batter'd heaven for mee,
Mild lambe, which with thy blood, hast mark'd the
        path;   10
Bright torch, which shin'st, that I the way may see,
Oh, with thine owne blood quench thine owne just wrath,
And if thy holy Spirit, my Muse did raise,
Deigne at my hands this crowne of prayer and praise.

Holy Sonnets

(1633)

DIVINE MEDITATIONS

1

As due by many titles I resigne
My selfe to thee, O God, first I was made
By thee, and for thee, and when I was decay'd
Thy blood bought that, the which before was thine,
I am thy sonne, made with thy selfe to shine,
Thy servant, whose paines thou hast still repaid,
Thy sheepe, thine Image, and till I betray'd
My selfe, a temple of thy Spirit divine;
Why doth the devill then usurpe in mee?
Why doth he steale, nay ravish that's thy right?   10
Except thou rise and for thine owne worke fight,
Oh I shall soone despaire, when I doe see
That thou lov'st mankind well, yet wilt'not chuse me,
And Satan hates mee, yet is loth to lose mee.   (II)

2

Oh my blacke Soule! now thou art summoned
By sicknesse, deaths herald, and champion;
Thou art like a pilgrim, which abroad hath done
Treason, and durst not turne to whence hee is fled,
Or like a thiefe, which till deaths doome be read,
Wisheth himselfe delivered from prison;
But damn'd and hal'd to execution,
Wisheth that still he might be imprisoned;
Yet grace, if thou repent, thou canst not lacke;
But who shall give thee that grace to beginne?   10
Oh make thy selfe with holy mourning blacke,
And red with blushing, as thou art with sinne,
Or wash thee in Christs blood, which hath this might
That being red, it dyes red soules to white.   (IV)

3

This is my playes last scene, here heavens appoint
My pilgrimages last mile; and my race

Idly, yet quickly runne, hath this last pace,
My spans last inch, my minutes last point,
And gluttonous death, will instantly unjoynt
My body, and soule, and I shall sleepe a space,
By my'ever-waking part shall see that face,
Whose feare already shakes my every joynt:
Then, as my soule, to'heaven her first seate, takes flight,
And earth-borne body, in the earth shall dwell,   10
So, fall my sinnes, that all may have their right,
To where they'are bred, and would presse me, to hell.
Impute me righteous, thus purg'd of evill,
For thus I leave the world, the flesh, and devill. (VI)

4

At the round earths imagin'd corners, blow
Your trumpets, Angells, and arise, arise
From death, you numberlesse infinities
Of soules, and to your scattred bodies goe,
All whom the flood did, and fire shall o'erthrow,
All whom warre, dearth, age, agues, tyrannies,
Despaire, law, chance, hath slaine, and you whose eyes,
Shall behold God, and never tast deaths woe.
But let them sleepe, Lord, and mee mourne a space,
For, if above all these, my sinnes abound,   10
'Tis late to aske abundance of thy grace,
When wee are there; here on this lowly ground,
Teach mee how to repent; for that's as good
As if thou'hadst seal'd my pardon, with thy blood.
(VII)

5

If poysonous mineralls, and if that tree,
Whose fruit threw death on else immortall us,
If lecherous goats, if serpents envious
Cannot be damn'd; Alas; why should I bee?
Why should intent or reason, borne in mee,
Make sinnes, else equall, in mee, more heinous?
And mercy being easie, and glorious
To God, in his sterne wrath, why threatens hee?
But who am I, that dare dispute with thee?

O God, Oh! of thine onely worthy blood,   10
And my teares, make a heavenly Lethean flood,
And drowne in it my sinnes blacke memorie.
That thou remember them, some claime as debt,
I thinke it mercy, if thou wilt forget.   (IX)

6

Death be not proud, though some have called thee
Mighty and dreadfull, for, thou art not soe,
For, those, whom thou think'st, thou dost overthrow,
Die not, poore death, nor yet canst thou kill mee;
From rest and sleepe, which but thy pictures bee,
Much pleasure, then from thee, much more must flow,
And soonest our best men with thee doe goe,
Rest of their bones, and soules deliverie.
Thou art slave to Fate, chance, kings, and desperate men,
And dost with poyson, warre, and sicknesse dwell,   10
And poppie, or charmes can make us sleepe as well,
And better then thy stroake; why swell'st thou then?
One short sleepe past, wee wake eternally,
And death shall be no more, Death thou shalt die. (X)

7

Spit in my face yee Jewes, and pierce my side,
Buffet, and scoffe, scourge, and crucifie mee,
For I have sinn'd, and sinn'd, and onely hee,
Who could do no iniquitie, hath dyed:
But by my death can not be satisfied
My sinnes, which passe the Jewes impiety:
They kill'd once an inglorious man, but I
Crucifie him daily, being now glorified.
Oh let mee then, his strange love still admire:
Kings pardon, but he bore our punishment.   10
And *Jacob* came cloth'd in vile harsh attire
But to supplant and with gainfull intent:
God cloth'd himselfe in vile mans flesh, that so
Hee might be weake enough to suffer woe.   (XI)

8

Why are wee by all creatures waited on?

Why doe the prodigall elements supply
Life and food to mee, being more pure then I,
Simple, and further from corruption?
Why brook'st thou, ignorant horse, subjection?
Why dost thou bull, and bore so seelily
Dissemble weaknesse, and by'one mans stroke die,
Whose whole kinde, you might swallow and feed upon?
Weaker I am, woe is mee, and worse then you,
You have not sinn'd, nor need be timorous.   10
But wonder at a greater wonder, for to us
Created nature doth these things subdue,
But their Creator, whom sin, nor nature tyed,
For us, his Creatures, and his foes, hath dyed. (XII)

9

What if this present were the worlds last night?
Marke in my heart, O Soule, where thou dost dwell,
The picture of Christ crucified, and tell
Whether that countenance can thee affright,
Teares in his eyes quench the amasing light,
Blood fills his frownes, which from his pierc'd head fell,
And can that tongue adjudge thee unto hell,
Which pray'd forgivenesse for his foes fierce spight?
No, no; but as in my idolatrie
I said to all my profane mistresses,   10
Beauty, of pitty, foulnesse onely is
A signe of rigour: so I say to thee,
To wicked spirits are horrid shapes assign'd,
This beauteous forme assures a pitious minde. (XIII)

10

Batter my heart, three person'd God; for, you
As yet but knocke, breathe, shine, and seeke to mend;
That I may rise, and stand, o'erthrow mee,'and bend
Your force, to breake, blowe, burn and make me new.
I, like an usurpt towne, to'another due,
Labour to'admit you, but Oh, to no end,
Reason your viceroy in mee, mee should defend,
But is captiv'd and proves weake or untrue,
Yet dearly'I love you, and would be lov'd faine,

But am betroth'd unto your enemie,   10
Divorce mee,'untie, or breake that knot againe,
Take mee to you, imprison mee, for I
Except you'enthrall mee, never shall be free,
Nor ever chast, except you ravish mee.   (XIV)

11

Wilt thou love God, as he thee! then digest,
My Soule, this wholsome meditation,
How God the Spirit, by Angels waited on
In heaven, doth make his Temple in thy brest,
The Father having begot a Sonne most blest,
And still begetting, (for he ne'r begonne)
Hath deign'd to chuse thee by adoption,
Coheire to'his glory,'and Sabbaths endlesse rest;
And as a robb'd man, which by search doth finde
His stolne stuffe sold, must lose or buy'it againe: 10
The Sonne of glory came downe, and was slaine,
Us whom he'had made, and Satan stolne, to unbinde.
'Twas much, that man was made like God before,
But, that God should be made like man, much more.
                                                                  (XV)

12

Father, part of his double interest
Unto thy kingdome, thy Sonne gives to mee,
His joynture in the knottie Trinitie,
Hee keepes, and gives mee his deaths conquest.
This Lambe, whose death, with life the world hath blest,
Was from the worlds beginning slaine, and he
Hath made two Wills, which with the Legacie
Of his and thy kingdome, doe thy Sonnes invest,
Yet such are those laws, that men argue yet
Whether a man those statutes can fulfill;   10
None doth, but all-healing grace and Spirit,
Revive againe what law and letter kill.
Thy lawes abridgement, and thy last command
Is all but love; Oh let that last Will stand!   (XVI)

(Holy Sonnets added in 1635)

DIVINE MEDITATIONS

1

Thou hast made me, And shall thy worke decay?
Repaire me now, for now mine end doth haste,
I runne to death, and death meets me as fast,
And all my pleasures are like yesterday,
I dare not move my dimme eyes any way,
Despaire behind, and death before doth cast
Such terrour, and my feebled flesh doth waste
By sinne in it, which it t'wards hell doth weigh;
Onely thou art above, and when towards thee
By thy leave I can looke, I rise againe;   10
But our old subtle foe so tempteth me,
That not one houre I can my selfe sustaine;
Thy Grace may wing me to prevent his art
And thou like Adamant draw mine iron heart.   (I)

2

I am a little world made cunningly
Of Elements, and an Angelike spright,
But black sinne hath betraid to endlesse night
My worlds both parts, and (oh) both parts must die.
You which beyond that heaven which was most high
Have found new sphears, and of new lands can write,
Powre new seas in mine eyes, that so I might
Drowne my world with my weeping earnestly,
Or wash it, if it must be drown'd no more:
But oh it must be burnt; alas the fire   10
Of lust and envie have burnt it heretofore,
And made it fouler; Let their flames retire,
And burne me ô Lord, with a fiery zeale
Of thee and thy house, which doth in eating heale. (v)

3

O might those sighes and teares returne againe
Into my breast and eyes, which I have spent,
That I might in this holy discontent

[Holy Sonnets] 156

Mourne with some fruit, as I have mourn'd in vaine;
In my Idolatry what showres of raine
Mine eyes did waste? what griefs my heart did rent?
That sufferance was my sinne, now I repent;
Because I did suffer I must suffer paine.
Th'hydroptique drunkard, and night-scouting thiefe,
The itchy Lecher, and selfe tickling proud   10
Have the remembrance of past joyes, for reliefe
Of comming ills. To (poore) me is allow'd
No ease; for, long, yet vehement griefe hath beene
Th'effect and cause, the punishment and sinne. (III)

4

If faithful soules be alike glorifi'd
As Angels, then my fathers soule doth see,
And adds this even to full felicitie,
That valiantly I hels wide mouth o'rstride:
But if our mindes to these soules be descry'd
By circumstances, and by signes that be
Apparent in us, not immediately,
How shall my mindes white truth to them be try'd?
They see idolatrous lovers weepe and mourne,
And vile blasphemous Conjurers to call   10
On Jesus name, and Pharisaicall
Dissemblers feigne devotion. Then turne
O pensive soule, to God, for he knowes best
Thy true griefe, for he put it in my breast.   (VIII)

(Holy Sonnets from the Westmoreland MS.)

1

Since she whome I lovd, hath payd her last debt
To Nature, and to hers, and my good is dead,
And her soule early into heaven ravished,
Wholy in heavenly things my mind is sett.
Here the admyring her my mind did whett
To seeke thee God; so streames do shew the head,
But though I have found thee, and thou my thirst hast
     fed,
A holy thirsty dropsy melts mee yett.

But why should I begg more love, when as thou
Dost wooe my soule, for hers offring all thine: 10
And dost not only feare least I allow
My love to saints and Angels, things divine,
But in thy tender jealosy dost doubt
Least the World, fleshe, yea Devill putt thee out.

(XVII)

2

Show me deare Christ, thy spouse, so bright and cleare.
What, is it she, which on the other shore
Goes richly painted? or which rob'd and tore
Laments and mournes in Germany and here?
Sleepes she a thousand, then peepes up one yeare?
Is she selfe truth and errs? now new, now outwore?
Doth she,'and did she, and shall she evermore
On one, on seaven, or on no hill appeare?
Dwells she with us, or like adventuring knights
First travaile we to seeke and then make love?   10
Betray kind husband thy spouse to our sights,
And let myne amorous soule court thy mild Dove,
Who is most trew, and pleasing to thee, then
When she'is embrac'd and open to most men. (XVIII)

3

Oh, to vex me, contraryes meete in one:
Inconstancy unnaturally hath begott
A constant habit; that when I would not
I change in vowes, and in devotione.
As humorous is my contritione
As my prophane love, and as soone forgott:
As ridlingly distemperd, cold and hott,
As praying, as mute; as infinite, as none.
I durst not view heaven yesterday; and to day
In prayers, and flattering speaches I court God: 10
To morrow I quake with true feare of his rod.
So my devout fitts come and go away
Like a fantastique Ague: save that here
Those are my best dayes, when I shake with feare.

(XIX)

A Litanie

I

THE FATHER

Father of Heaven, and him, by whom
It, and us for it, and all else, for us
   Thou madest, and govern'st ever, come
And re-create mee, now growne ruinous:
      My heart is by dejection, clay,
      And by selfe-murder, red.
From this red earth, O Father, purge away
All vicious tinctures, that new fashioned
I may rise up from death, before I'am dead.

II

THE SONNE

O Sonne of God, who seeing two things,   10
Sinne, and death crept in, which were never made,
   By bearing one, tryed'st that what stings
The other could thine heritage invade;
      O be thou nail'd unto my heart,
      And crucified againe,
Part not from it, though it from thee would part,
But let it be by applying so thy paine,
Drown'd in thy blood, and in thy passion slaine.

III

THE HOLY GHOST

O Holy Ghost, whose temple I
Am, but of mudde walls, and condensed dust,   20
   And being sacrilegiously
Halfe wasted with youths fires, of pride and lust,
      Must with new stormes be weatherbeat;
      Double in my heart thy flame,
Which let devout sad teares intend; and let
(Though this glasse lanthorne, flesh, do suffer maime)
Fire, Sacrifice, Priest, Altar be the same.

IV

THE TRINITY

O Blessed glorious Trinity,
Bones to Philosophy, but milke to faith,
  Which, as wise serpents, diversly   30
Most slipperinesse, yet most entanglings hath,
      As you distinguish'd undistinct
      By power, love, knowledge bee,
Give mee a such selfe different instinct,
Of these let all mee elemented bee,
Of power, to love, to know, you unnumbred three.

V

THE VIRGIN MARY

For that faire blessed Mother-maid,
Whose flesh redeem'd us; That she-Cherubin,
  Which unlock'd Paradise, and made
One claime for innocence, and disseiz'd sinne,   40
      Whose wombe was a strange heav'n, for there
      God cloath'd himselfe, and grew,
Our zealous thankes wee poure. As her deeds were
Our helpes, so are her prayers; nor can she sue
In vaine, who hath such titles unto you.

VI

THE ANGELS

And since this life our nonage is,
And wee in Wardship to thine Angels be,
  Native in heavens faire Palaces
Where we shall be but denizen'd by thee,
      As th'earth conceiving by the Sunne,   50
      Yeelds faire diversitie,
Yet never knowes which course that light doth run,
So let mee study, that mine actions bee
Worthy their sight, though blinde in how they see.

THE PATRIARCHES

And let thy Patriarches Desire
(Those great Grandfathers, of thy Church, which saw
  More in the cloud, then wee in fire,
Whom Nature clear'd more, then us grace and law,
     And now in Heaven still pray, that wee
     May use our new helpes right,)   60
Be satisfied, and fructifie in mee;
Let not my minde be blinder by more light
Nor Faith by Reason added, lose her sight.

VIII

THE PROPHETS

Thy Eagle-sighted Prophets too,
Which were thy Churches Organs, and did sound
  That harmony, which made of two
One law, and did unite, but not confound;
     Those heavenly Poëts which did see
     Thy will, and it expresse
In rythmique feet, in common pray for mee,   70
That I by them excuse not my excesse
In seeking secrets, or Poëtiquenesse.

IX

THE APOSTLES

And thy illustrious Zodiacke
Of twelve Apostles, which ingirt this All,
  (From whom whosever do not take
Their light, to darke deep pits, throw downe, and fall,)
     As through their prayers, thou'hast let mee know
     That their bookes are divine;
May they pray still, and be heard, that I goe
Th'old broad way in applying; O decline   80
Mee, when my comment would make thy word mine.

X

THE MARTYRS

And since thou so desirously
Did'st long to die, that long before thou could'st,
  And long since thou no more couldst dye,
Thou in thy scatter'd mystique body wouldst
      In Abel dye, and ever since
      In thine, let their blood come
To begge for us, a discreet patience
Of death, or of worse life: for Oh, to some
Not to be Martyrs, is a martyrdome.   90

XI

THE CONFESSORS

Therefore with thee triumpheth there
A Virgin Squadron of white Confessors,
  Whose bloods betroth'd, not marryed were,
Tender'd, not taken by those Ravishers:
      They know, and pray, that wee may know,
      In every Christian
Hourly tempestuous persecutions grow,
Tentations martyr us alive; A man
Is to himselfe a Dioclesian.

XII

THE VIRGINS

Thy cold white snowie Nunnery,   100
Which, as thy mother, their high Abbesse, sent
  Their bodies backe againe to thee,
As thou hadst lent them, cleane and innocent,
      Though they have not obtain'd of thee,
      That or thy Church, or I,
Should keep, as they, our first integrity;
Divorce thou sinne in us, or bid it die,
And call chast widowhead Virginitie.

XIII

THE DOCTORS

Thy sacred Academe above
Of Doctors, whose paines have unclasp'd, and taught 110
    Both bookes of life to us (for love
To know thy Scriptures tells us, we are wrought
        In thy other booke) pray for us there
        That what they have misdone
Or mis-said, wee to that may not adhere;
Their zeale may be our sinne. Lord let us runne
Meane waies, and call them stars, but not the Sunne.

XIV

And whil'st this universall Quire,
That Church in triumph, this in warfare here,
    Warm'd with one all-partaking fire   120
Of love, that none be lost, which cost thee deare,
        Pray ceaslesly, and thou hearken too,
        (Since to be gratious
Our taske is treble, to pray, beare, and doe)
Heare this prayer Lord, O Lord deliver us
From trusting in those prayers, though powr'd out thus.

XV

From being anxious, or secure,
Dead clods of sadnesse, or light squibs of mirth,
    From thinking, that great courts immure
All, or no happinesse, or that this earth   130
        Is only for our prison fram'd,
        Or that thou art covetous
To them whom thou lov'st, or that they are maim'd
From reaching this worlds sweet, who seek thee thus,
With all their might, Good Lord deliver us.

XVI

From needing danger, to bee good,
From owing thee yesterdaies teares to day,

From trusting so much to thy blood,
That in that hope, wee wound our soule away,
   From bribing thee with Almes, to excuse   140
     Some sinne more burdenous,
From light affecting, in religion, newes,
From thinking us all soule, neglecting thus
Our mutuall duties, Lord deliver us.

   XVII

From tempting Satan to tempt us,
By our connivence, or slack companie,
   From measuring ill by vitious,
Neglecting to choake sins spawne, Vanitie,
     From indiscreet humilitie,
     Which might be scandalous,   150
And cast reproach on Christianitie,
From being spies, or to spies pervious,
From thirst, or scorne of fame, deliver us.

   XVIII

Deliver us for thy descent
Into the Virgin, whose wombe was a place
   Of middle kind; and thou being sent
To'ungratious us, staid'st at her full of grace,
     And through thy poore birth, where first thou
     Glorifiedst Povertie,
And yet soone after riches didst allow,   160
By accepting Kings gifts in the Epiphanie
Deliver, and make us, to both waies free.

   XIX

And through that bitter agonie,
Which is still the agonie of pious wits,
   Disputing what distorted thee,
And interrupted evennesse, with fits,
     And through thy free confession
     Though thereby they were then
Made blind, so that thou might'st from them have gone,
Good Lord deliver us, and teach us when   170
Wee may not, and we may blinde unjust men.

XX

Through thy submitting all, to blowes
Thy face, thy clothes to spoile, thy fame to scorne,
   All waies, which rage, or Justice knowes,
And by which thou could'st shew, that thou wast born,
      And through thy gallant humblenesse
      Which thou in death did'st shew,
Dying before thy soule they could expresse,
Deliver us from death, by dying so,
To this world, ere this world doe bid us goe.   180

XXI

When senses, which thy souldiers are,
Wee arme against thee, and they fight for sinne,
   When want, sent but to tame, doth warre
And worke despaire a breach to enter in,
      When plenty, Gods image, and seale
      Makes us Idolatrous,
And love it, not him, whom it should reveale,
When wee are mov'd to seeme religious
Only to vent wit, Lord deliver us.

XXII

In Churches, when the'infirmitie   190
Of him that speakes, diminishes the Word,
   When Magistrates doe mis-apply
To us, as we judge, lay or ghostly sword,
      When plague, which is thine Angell, raignes,
      Or wars, thy Champions, swaie,
When Heresie, thy second deluge, gaines;
In th'houre of death, the'Eve of last judgement day,
Deliver us from the sinister way.

XXIII

Heare us, O heare us Lord; to thee
A sinner is more musique, when he prayes,   200
   Then spheares, or Angels praises bee,
In Panegyrique Allelujaes,

Heare us, for till thou heare us, Lord
We know not what to say.
Thine eare to'our sighes, teares, thoughts gives voice and
word.
O Thou who Satan heard'st in Jobs sicke day,
Heare thy selfe now, for thou in us dost pray.

XXIV

That wee may change to evennesse
This intermitting aguish Pietie,
That snatching cramps of wickednesse   210
And Apoplexies of fast sin, may die;
That musique of thy promises
Not threats in Thunder may
Awaken us to our just offices;
What in thy booke, thou dost, or creatures say,
That we may heare, Lord heare us, when wee pray.

XXV

That our eares sicknesse wee may cure,
And rectifie those Labyrinths aright,
That wee by harkning, not procure
Our praise, nor others dispraise so invite,   220
That wee get not a slipperinesse,
And senslesly decline,
From hearing bold wits jeast at Kings excesse,
To'admit the like of majestie divine,
That we may locke our eares, Lord open thine.

XXVI

That living law, the Magistrate,
Which to give us, and make us physicke, doth
Our vices often aggravate,
That Preachers taxing sinne, before her growth,
That Satan, and invenom'd men   230
Which well, if we starve, dine,
When they doe most accuse us, may see then
Us, to amendment, heare them; thee decline;
That we may open our eares, Lord lock thine.

XXVII

That learning, thine Ambassador,
From thine allegeance wee never tempt,
   That beauty, paradises flower
For physicke made, from poyson be exempt,
      That wit, borne apt, high good to doe,
        By dwelling lazily   240
On Natures nothing, be not nothing too,
That our affections kill us not, nor dye,
Heare us, weake ecchoes, O thou eare, and cry.

XXVIII

Sonne of God heare us, and since thou
By taking our blood, owest it us againe,
   Gaine to thy selfe, or us allow;
And let not both us and thy selfe be slaine;
      O lambe of God, which took'st our sinne
        Which could not stick to thee,
O let it not returne to us againe,   250
But Patient and Physition being free,
As sinne is nothing, let it no where be.

The Crosse

Since Christ embrac'd the Crosse it selfe, dare I
His image, th'image of his Crosse deny?
Would I have profit by the sacrifice,
And dare the chosen Altar to despise?
It bore all other sinnes, but is it fit
That it should beare the sinne of scorning it?
Who from the picture would avert his eye,
How would he flye his paines, who there did dye?
From mee, no Pulpit, nor misgrounded law,
Nor scandall taken, shall this Crosse withdraw,   10
It shall not, for it cannot; for, the losse
Of this Crosse, were to mee another Crosse;
Better were worse, for, no affliction,

No Crosse is so extreme, as to have none.
Who can blot out the Crosse, which th'instrument
Of God, dew'd on mee in the Sacrament?
Who can deny mee power, and liberty
To stretch mine armes, and mine owne Crosse to be?
Swimme, and at every stroake, thou art thy Crosse,
The Mast and yard make one, where seas do tosse.   20
Looke down, thou spiest out Crosses in small things;
Looke up, thou seest birds rais'd on crossed wings;
All the Globes frame, and spheares, is nothing else
But the Meridians crossing Parallels.
Materiall Crosses then, good physicke bee,
And yet spirituall have chiefe dignity.
These for extracted chimique medicine serve,
And cure much better, and as well preserve;
Then are you your own physicke, or need none,
When Still'd, or purg'd by tribulation.   30
For when that Crosse ungrudg'd, unto you stickes,
Then are you to your selfe, a Crucifixe.
As perchance, Carvers do not faces make,
But that away, which hid them there, do take:
Let Crosses, soe, take what hid Christ in thee,
And be his image, or not his, but hee.
But, as oft Alchimists doe coyners prove,
So may a selfe-dispising, get selfe-love.
And then as worst surfets, of best meates bee,
Soe is pride, issued from humility,   40
For, 'tis no child, but monster; therefore Crosse
Your joy in crosses, else, 'tis double losse.
And crosse thy senses, else, both they, and thou
Must perish soone, and to destruction bowe.
For if th'eye seeke good objects, and will take
No crosse from bad, wee cannot scape a snake.
So with harsh, hard, sowre, stinking, crosse the rest,
Make them indifferent; call nothing best.
But most the eye needs crossing, that can rome,
And move; To th'others th'objects must come home.   50
And crosse thy heart: for that in man alone
Points downewards, and hath palpitation.
Crosse those dejections, when it downeward tends,

And when it to forbidden heights pretends.
And as thy braine through bony walls doth vent
By sutures, which a Crosses forme present,
So when thy braine workes, ere thou utter it,
Crosse and correct concupiscence of witt.
Be covetous of Crosses, let none fall.
Crosse no man else, but crosse thy selfe in all.   60
Then doth the Crosse of Christ worke fruitfully
Within our hearts, when wee love harmlessly
That Crosses pictures much, and with more care
That Crosses children, which our Crosses are.

Upon the Annunciation and Passion
falling upon one day, 1608

Tamely fraile body,'abstaine to day; to day
My soule eates twice, Christ hither and away.
Shee sees him man, so like God made in this,
That of them both a circle embleme is,
Whose first and last concurre; this doubtfull day
Of feast or fast, Christ came, and went away;
Shee sees him nothing twice at once, who'is all;
Shee sees a Cedar plant it selfe, and fall,
Her Maker put to making, and the head
Of life, at once, not yet alive, and dead;   10
She sees at once the virgin mother stay
Reclus'd at home, Publique at Golgotha.
Sad and rejoyc'd shee's seen at once, and seen
At almost fiftie, and at scarce fifteene.
At once a Sonne is promis'd her, and gone,
Gabriell gives Christ to her, He her to John;
Not fully a mother, Shee's in Orbitie,
At once receiver and the legacie;
All this, and all betweene, this day hath showne,
Th'Abridgement of Christs story, which makes one   20
(As in plaine Maps, the furthest West is East)
Of the'Angels *Ave*,'and *Consummatum est*.
How well the Church, Gods Court of faculties
Deales, in some times, and seldome joyning these;

As by the selfe-fix'd Pole wee never doe
Direct our course, but the next starre thereto,
Which showes where the'other is, and which we say
(Because it strayes not farre) doth never stray;
So God by his Church, neerest to him, wee know,
And stand firme, if wee by her motion goe;   30
His Spirit, as his fiery Pillar doth
Leade, and his Church, as cloud; to one end both:
This Church, by letting these daies joyne, hath shown
Death and conception in mankinde is one:
Or 'twas in him the same humility,
That he would be a man, and leave to be:
Or as creation he had made, as God,
With the last judgement, but one period,
His imitating Spouse would joyne in one
Manhoods extremes: He shall come, he is gone: 40
Or as though one blood drop, which thence did fall,
Accepted, would have serv'd, he yet shed all;
So though the least of his paines, deeds, or words,
Would busie a life, she all this day affords;
This treasure then, in grosse, my Soule uplay,
And in my life retaile it every day.

Goodfriday, 1613. Riding Westward

Let mans Soule be a Spheare, and then, in this,
The intelligence that moves, devotion is,
And as the other Spheares, by being growne
Subject to forraigne motions, lose their owne,
And being by others hurried every day,
Scarce in a yeare their naturall forme obey:
Pleasure or businesse, so, our Soules admit
For their first mover, and are whirld by it.
Hence is't, that I am carryed towards the West
This day, when my Soules forme bends toward the East.
There I should see a Sunne, by rising set,   11
And by that setting endlesse day beget;
But that Christ on this Crosse, did rise and fall,
Sinne had eternally benighted all.

Yet dare I'almost be glad, I do not see
That spectacle of too much weight for mee.
Who sees Gods face, that is selfe life, must dye;
What a death were it then to see God dye?
It made his owne Lieutenant Nature shrinke,
It made his footstoole crack, and the Sunne winke.   20
Could I behold those hands which span the Poles,
And tune all spheares at once, pierc'd with those holes?
Could I behold that endlesse height which is
Zenith to us, and to'our Antipodes,
Humbled below us? or that blood which is
The seat of all our Soules, if not of his,
Make durt of dust, or that flesh which was worne
By God, for his apparell, rag'd, and torne?
If on these things I durst not looke, durst I
Upon his miserable mother cast mine eye,   30
Who was Gods partner here, and furnish'd thus
Halfe of that Sacrifice, which ransom'd us?
Though these things, as I ride, be from mine eye,
They, are present yet unto my memory,
For that looks towards them; and thou look'st towards mee,
O Saviour, as thou hang'st upon the tree;
I turne my backe to thee, but to receive
Corrections, till thy mercies bid thee leave.
O thinke mee worth thine anger, punish mee,
Burne off my rusts, and my deformity,   40
Restore thine Image, so much, by thy grace,
That thou may'st know mee, and I'll turne my face.

To Mr. Tilman after he had taken orders

Thou, whose diviner soule hath caus'd thee now
To put thy hand unto the holy Plough,
Making Lay-scornings of the Ministry,
Not an impediment, but victory;
What bringst thou home with thee? how is thy mind
Affected in the vintage? Dost thou finde
New thoughts and stirrings in thee? and as Steele
Toucht with a Loadstone, dost new motions feele?

Or, as a Ship after much paine and care,
For Iron and Cloth brings home rich Indian ware,   10
Hast thou thus traffiqu'd, but with farre more gaine
Of noble goods, and with lesse time and paine?
Art thou the same materials, as before,
Onely the stampe is changed; but no more? '
And as new crowned Kings alter the face,
But not the monies substance; so hath grace
Chang'd onely Gods old Image by Creation,
To Christs new stampe, at this thy Coronation?
Or, as we paint Angels with wings, because
They beare Gods message, and proclaime his lawes,   20
Since thou must doe the like, and so must move,
Art thou new feather'd with coelestiall love?
Deare, tell me where thy purchase lies, and shew
What thy advantage is above, below.
But if thy gayning doe surmount expression,
Why doth the foolish world scorne that profession,
Whose joyes passe speech? Why do they think unfit
That Gentry should joyne families with it?
Would they thinke it well if the day were spent
In dressing, Mistressing and complement?   30
Alas poore joyes, but poorer men, whose trust
Seems richly placed in refined dust;
(For, such are cloathes and beauties, which though gay,
Are, at the best, but as sublimed clay.)
Let then the world thy calling disrespect,
But goe thou on, and pitty their neglect.
What function is so noble, as to bee
Embassadour to God and destinie?
To open life, to give kingdomes to more
Than Kings give dignities; to keepe heavens doore?   40
Maries prerogative was to beare Christ, so
'Tis preachers to convey him, for they doe
As Angels out of clouds, from Pulpits speake;
And blesse the poore beneath, the lame, the weake.
If then th'Astronomers, whereas they spie
A new-found Starre, their Opticks magnifie,
How brave are those, who with their Engines, can
Bring man to heaven, and heaven againe to man?

These are thy titles and preheminences,
In whom must meet Gods graces, mens offences,   50
And so the heavens which beget all things here,
And the earth our mother, which these things doth beare,
Both these in thee, are in thy Calling knit,
And make thee now a blest Hermaphrodite.

A Hymne to Christ, at the
Authors last going into Germany

In what torne ship soever I embarke,
That ship shall be my embleme of thy Arke;
What sea soever swallow mee, that flood
Shall be to mee an embleme of thy blood;
Though thou with clouds of anger do disguise
Thy face; yet through that maske I know those eyes,
   Which, though they turne away sometimes,
      They never will despise.

I sacrifice this Iland unto thee,
And all whom I lov'd there, and who lov'd mee;   10
When I have put our seas twixt them and mee,
Put thou thy sea betwixt my sinnes and thee.
As the trees sap doth seeke the root below
In winter, in my winter now I goe,
   Where none but thee, th'Eternall root
      Of true Love I may know.

Nor thou nor thy religion dost controule,
The amorousnesse of an harmonious Soule,
But thou would'st have that love thy selfe: As thou
Art jealous, Lord, so I am jealous now,   20
Thou lov'st not, till from loving more, thou free
My soule: Who ever gives, takes libertie:
   O, if thou car'st not whom I love
      Alas, thou lov'st not mee.

Seale then this bill of my Divorce to All,
On whom those fainter beames of love did fall;

Marry those loves, which in youth scattered bee
On Fame, Wit, Hopes (false mistresses) to thee.
Churches are best for Prayer, that have least light:
To see God only, I goe out of sight: 30
   And to scape stormy dayes, I chuse
      An Everlasting night.

Hymne to God my God, in my sicknesse

Since I am comming to that Holy roome,
   Where, with thy Quire of Saints for evermore,
I shall be made thy Musique; As I come
   I tune the Instrument here at the dore,
   And what I must doe then, thinke now before.

Whilst my Physitians by their love are growne
   Cosmographers, and I their Mapp, who lie
Flat on this bed, that by them may be showne
   That this is my South-west discoverie
   Per fretum febris, by these streights to die,   10

I joy, that in these straits, I see my West;
   For, though theire currants yeeld returne to none,
What shall my West hurt me? As West and East
   In all flatt Maps (and I am one) are one,
   So death doth touch the Resurrection.

Is the Pacifique Sea my home? Or are
   The Easterne riches? Is *Jerusalem*?
Anyan, and *Magellan,* and *Gibraltare,*
   All streights, and none but streights, are wayes to them,
   Whether where *Japhet* dwelt, or *Cham,* or *Sem.*   20

We thinke that *Paradise* and *Calvarie,*
   Christs Crosse, and *Adams* tree, stood in one place;
Looke Lord, and finde both *Adams* met in me;
   As the first *Adams* sweat surrounds my face,
   May the last *Adams* blood my soule embrace.

[*Hymne to God my God, in my sicknesse*]   174

So, in his purple wrapp'd receive mee Lord,
    By these his thornes give me his other Crowne;
And as to others soules I preach'd thy word,
    Be this my Text, my Sermon to mine owne,
        Therfore that he may raise the Lord throws down.   30

A Hymne to God the Father

I

Wilt thou forgive that sinne where I begunne,
    Which is my sin, though it were done before?
Wilt thou forgive those sinnes through which I runne,
    And doe them still: though still I doe deplore?
        When thou hast done, thou hast not done,
            For, I have more.

II

Wilt thou forgive that sinne by which I wonne
    Others to sinne? and, made my sinne their doore?
Wilt thou forgive that sinne which I did shunne
    A yeare, or two: but wallowed in, a score?   10
        When thou hast done, thou hast not done,
            For, I have more.

III

I have a sinne of feare, that when I have spunne
    My last thred, I shall perish on the shore;
Sweare by thy selfe, that at my death thy Sunne
    Shall shine as it shines now, and heretofore;
        And, having done that, Thou hast done,
            I have no more.

Notes

SONGS AND SONETS

These cannot be dated with any accuracy, though Jonson affirmed Donne "to have written all his best pieces ere he was twenty-five years old," and it is now generally assumed that most (but not all) of them were written before the turn of the century. Gosse assumed that the more lusty and cynical of the poems were written in his unattached youth, the more constant and tender after his meeting with Anne More, his future wife, in 1598; but few now would be disposed to convict him of so orderly a procedure. Only for *A Valediction: forbidding mourning* is there solid external evidence for a date: Walton says in his *Life* that it was written to his wife on his departure for France with Sir Robert Drury in 1611.

"Sonets" is of course used not of the fourteen-line form, but in the Elizabethan sense of any short amatory poem.

THE GOOD-MORROW

Line 18: the constant and matched worlds of our love (a favorite figure with Donne) are contrasted to the biting cold of the Northern, the declining sun of the Western hemispheres.

SONG

Line 2: the forked root of the mandrake was thought to resemble the human form.

THE SUNNE RISING

Line 17: *both the'India's*: East and West. *Of . . . Myne*: especially gold, silver, and precious stone.
  Line 24: *alchimie*: fraudulent conversion.

LOVES USURY

Line 5: the poem appeals for the reign of body and lust over the reign of love.

THE CANONIZATION

The title provides the central image, and is, as often with Donne, to be taken quite literally: the lovers are *canonized,* i.e. made saints, and therefore may be asked to intercede for later lovers, to beg from above a pattern of their love.

Line 7: be a courtier or a merchant (the king's face was stamped on coins).

Lines 19-27: *we* prove the truth of what have been only literary conventions (*Tapers*; the Eagle and the Dove; the *Phoenix*: a bird fabled to rise anew from the ashes of his funeral pyre).

THE LEGACIE

The fantastic logic of this poem is based on the old convention of lovers' exchanging hearts; its shock comes from the literal and extreme visualization of its working out, which also lends itself to the wry, skeptical turns.

A FEAVER

Lines 13-16: she being "the worlds soule," her fever is the holocaust at the Last Judgment.

AIRE AND ANGELS

This extremely subtle poem is, like *The Extasie,* a meditation on the relation of soul and body in love; its principal image parallels the Scholastic paradoxes about the embodiment of Angels (pure spirit) in corporeal form.

BREAKE OF DAY

The difficulties of this poem are largely removed if one perceives, as Grierson points out, that it is addressed by a woman to her lover (unusual in Donne), not *vice versa.* The poem is traditionally an *aubade,* a song at morning parting.

THE ANNIVERSARIE

Line 22: we alone on earth are "thoroughly blest"; in heaven all will be.

A VALEDICTION: OF MY NAME, IN THE WINDOW

All four Valedictions are poems of parting.

Stanza II: glass may be either transparent or a reflecting mirror.

Stanza VI: in astrology, stars in their "supremacie" are said to determine character.

TWICKNAM GARDEN

Again an extravagant and ironic development of an old Petrarchan idea: the disproportion between the despair of the lover and the gaiety of the burgeoning garden.

A VALEDICTION: OF THE BOOKE

Another variation on the theme of the lovers as epitomes, or complete worlds in themselves. Note how successive stanzas parallel to the epitomizing lovers the worlds of the scholars, the divines, the lawyers, and the statesmen. The witty intricacies of the demonstration are paraphrased in Grierson's notes.

Line 3: *Esloygne*: from Old French *esloignier*, to remove to a distance.

Lines 7-9: Corinna, Polla Argentaria (his wife), and Helena (or Phantasia), who were reputed to have inspired respectively Pindar, Lucan, and Homer.

Lines 59-61: longitudes could theoretically be computed by measuring the difference in time of eclipses at different points, though the method was not exactly practical. In the analogy, "the darke eclipses" are of course her absence, and the longitudes "how long this love will bee."

LOVES GROWTH

Line 18: stars that shine in the daylight are not made larger, but are shown to be more "eminent" than their invisible fellows.

THE DREAME

The dream of the loved one is a traditional Petrarachan theme; Donne characteristically turns it to reality. Cf. Mario Praz in *The Flaming Heart*.

A VALEDICTION: OF WEEPING

See William Empson's provocative analysis in *Seven Types of Ambiguity*.

LOVES ALCHYMIE

Lines 7-10: "Th'Elixar" is the universal cure for both disease and death, unavailingly sought by the "chymique" or alchemist, who nevertheless boasts of the incidental sensations or stimulants. Donne's implied parallel with love is exact.

Line 15: *my man*: my servant.

THE FLEA

Apparently the most popular of Donne's poems in his own century; it was placed first in the 1635–1669 editions. Perhaps therefore some more particular indication of what his contemporaries meant by Donne's wit. Note that it is a version of a recurrent Elizabethan lyric subject, Persuasions to a Mistress.

A NOCTURNALL UPON S. LUCIES DAY

The poem may play upon the name of Donne's friend and patroness, Lucy, Countess of Bedford. If so it must be late, possibly written at the time of her serious illness in 1612. Its extravagant protestations are compatible with the mode of the times, though they reflect upon the attempt to take his poems as literal autobiography.

Line 21: *limbecke*: the alchemist's device for distilling.

Lines 37-40: at its shortest day the sun begins to renew itself; it also (Dec. 21st) runs into the zodiacal sign of Capricorn, the Goat, the symbol of lust.

THE BAITE

A variation on Marlowe's popular *Passionate shepherd to his love*. See introduction.

A VALEDICTION: FORBIDDING MOURNING

Whether or not, as Walton says, addressed to his wife in 1611, this is the most assured in feeling of the four Valedictions. The compass image in the last three stanzas is a *locus classicus* for the metaphysical conceit.

Lines 9-12: earthquakes as against the slow, swinging motion of the Ninth Sphere, which in the Ptolemaic astronomy accounted for the precession of the equinoxes.

Line 13: *sublunary*: subject to the moon's influence, changeable.

THE EXTASIE

The poem is both a Persuasion to Love, and a highly intricate argument about (as Grierson says) "Donne's metaphysic of love, the interconnexion and mutual dependence of body and soul." The mixture is both characteristic and unique.

"Ecstasy" is the technical term for the state of mystical communion with God, the Absolute. As Plotinus wrote, it is marked by "a simplification, an abandonment of self, a perfect quietude, a desire of contact, in short a wish to merge oneself." These stages may be found in the poem, especially lines 15-35.

Line 52: Scholastic philosophy held that the celestial spheres were governed by guiding Angels, pure incorporeal Intelligences.

Lines 61-64: contemporary physiology explained the continuing mystery of the power of mind over body by the intervention of a "spirituous fluid," sometimes identified with the blood.

LOVES DIET

Line 25: the buzzard, though a hawk, and so usable by Falconers, had a name for being clumsy, stupid, blind, and feeding on carrion (his dead love). The multiple meanings are characteristic.

THE WILL

Line 3: Argus had a hundred eyes.

Line 10: among the celestial bodies, the planets were regarded as particularly eccentric.

Lines 19-20: Catholics approved the value of good works for salvation; the Schismaticks (more extreme Protestants) allowed only faith.

Line 39: *Bedlam*: Bethlehem Hospital, the London insane asylum.

THE FUNERALL

"That subtile wreath of haire" is of course not his own, but a gift of his love's ("a better braine").

THE PRIMROSE

A very numerological poem. The perfect primrose (a symbol of woman) has five petals; to have four or six is to be less or more than woman, either deplorable. Further speculations play upon the ancient Pythagorean thesis that number deciphered is the key to truth.

THE RELIQUE

The poem may have been addressed to Lady Magdalen Herbert, George Herbert's mother, in which case lines 17-18 involve a play on her name.

Line 28: The kiss of salutation *at* meals was customary and quite compatible with a chaste relationship.

THE DAMPE

Line 21: To die in contemporary slang meant to reach sexual consummation; the love poets frequently play on it.

Line 24: Here I have ventured against Grierson's authority to restore the 1635–1669 reading: "Naked" seems simply more vigorous and Donne-like than "In that."

THE DISSOLUTION

Lines 9-10: the four basic elements were considered fire, air, water, and earth.

A JEAT RING SENT

The ring has been sent by the mistress to the lover who speaks.

THE PROHIBITION

Line 19: cf. note on *The Dampe*, line 21.

FAREWELL TO LOVE

Line 10: against most textual authority, and Grierson, I have preferred "rise" to "sise" as making more balanced sense.

Line 12: presumably a gilt gingerbread man from a fair.

Line 30: here Grierson, without textual authority, amended to ("Eagers desire"); I cannot see the improvement and have restored the reading of the early texts. The passage is puzzling because the syntax compresses two ideas into one: desire is nature's spur "to raise posterity," but its brevity is her demonstration that the act of love is not an end in itself.

EPIGRAMS

The aims of epigrams are brevity and pointed turn; Donne's are among his "evaporations of wit." They must be of various dates: *A lame begger* probably dates from the time of the Cadiz expedition, while *Raderus* must be after 1602, since in that year Matthew Rader, a German Jesuit, published an expurgated edition of Martial. The epigram is therefore also a hit at the Jesuits, a favorite target for Donne.

ELEGIES

Except for *The Autumnall* (q. v.) the Elegies cannot be accurately dated, though of course the cynical and sensual tone of most suggests an early date, probably before 1600. It is my own notion that in title, in subject matter, and in the harsh colloquialism of diction and meter they owe much to Marlowe's rough translation of Ovid's *Amores*, published with Sir John David's Epigrams about 1596, but certainly at large in MS earlier.

I JEALOSIE

Line 6: *crocheting*: playing in quick time, from crotchet, a quarter note.

VII "NATURES LAY IDEOT"

Lines 13, 15, 17: *since*: the time when.

IX THE AUTUMNALL

Probably addressed around 1607–1609 to Lady Magdalen
Herbert, then somewhat over forty, the widowed mother
of ten children, and by the standards of the time an elderly
(but not "antique") woman. Compare *The Relique*.

Line 10: *Tropique clyme*: the climate of the Tropics
of Cancer and Capricorn, 23 degrees *away* from the equa-
tor.

Line 16: *Anachorit*: anchorite, hermit.

Line 47: *lation*: motion.

XII HIS PARTING FROM HER

Night is addressed in lines 1-12, Love in 13-40, his mistress thereafter.

XVI ON HIS MISTRIS

The poet dissuades his mistress from following him in the
guise of a page—a favorite plot of the romances and plays,
of which *As You Like It* and *Twelfth Night* are variants.

Line 37: Grierson thought this the true reading of the
line, but on grounds of taste substituted an alternate
which suppressed the blunt second usage of "know."

Line 44: *Gallerie*: entrance hall or corridor.

XVIII LOVES PROGRESS

Lines 47-52: according to ancient cosmographers, the
first meridian of longitude passed through the Canary
Islands.

Line 58: *Remora*: this odd image is based on the fact
that Remora (teeth, pearls) are fish that attach themselves
to larger ones by means of suction disks on the tops of
their heads.

Line 96: *Clyster*: an enema.

XIX GOING TO BED

Line 4: *standing*: a pun; compare line 24.

Line 36: Hippomenes won in a footrace the hand of the fleet Atalanta by dropping on the course for her temptation three golden apples from the garden of the Hesperides given him by Aphrodite. Donne has reversed the story.

EPITHALAMION MADE AT LINCOLNES INNE

Presumably made while Donne was a student at Lincoln's Inn, 1592–1594. Lincoln's Inn was (and is) one of the Inns of Court, London's law schools, accommodating not only budding lawyers but "frolique Patricians" pursuing a course of nominal study and much play (cf. line 30). This poem, with its astringent mixture of mockery, irony, shock, and genuine emotion, may be instructively contrasted with Spenser's harmoniously beautiful *Epithalamion*.

Line 12: *perfection*: retaining much of its root of accomplishment of appointed end, and also in implicit paradox with the Pauline ideal of chastity as the perfection of woman.

Lines 15-16: *Angels*: also Elizabethan gold coins.

Line 26: *Sonnes*: punning on "suns." The whole stanza satirizes the nobles—of whom, no doubt this bridegroom is one—who in marrying the daughters of rich citizens for money drink up "wealths deep oceans."

Line 57: *nill*: will not.

SATYRE III "KIND PITTY CHOKES MY SPLEENE"

Probably written around 1595. Recall that Donne, though later an Anglican Dean, was raised as a Roman Catholic.

Lines 96-97: presumably Philip of Spain, some Pope Gregory, Henry VIII, and Luther—respectively Catholic and Protestant secular and religious leaders.

LETTERS TO SEVERALL PERSONAGES

In the fashion of the time, the familiar letters combine matter and personal eulogy, though I have not chosen the more ingenious and extravagant examples of the latter.

THE STORME

This, and its companion piece *The Calme,* were written during Essex's Azores expedition in 1597. Christopher Brooke was Donne's chamber-fellow at Lincoln's Inn, and a poet. Note that the "thou" used throughout is the form of intimate address.

Lines 13-16: winds were supposed to arise from exhalations of the earth and to rebound from the frozen middle regions of the air.

Line 33: *Jonas:* Jonah.

THE CALME

Lines 3-4: in Aesop's fable, the frogs received as king from Jupiter first a block of wood, and then, at their protest, a stork who ate them.

Lines 17-18: lanterns in the ships' high sterns were used to keep them together when sailing at night. Jonson to Drummond particularly admired the lines about feathers and dust.

Line 23: *Calenture:* a fever inducing a delirium which caused sailors to fancy the ocean a green field into which they leaped.

Line 28: Shadrach, Meshach, and Abednego in the fiery furnace.

Line 33: compare Marlowe's *Tamburlaine.*

Lines 35-38: a pestilence of ants devoured the Emperor Tiberius's pet snake, and drove him back from the gates of Rome. So the enemy's galleys, oar-driven by prisoners, may consume our sailing pinnaces.

TO SIR HENRY WOTTON: ("Sir, more than kisses")

This, according to Grierson, is Donne's contribution to a fashionable literary debate, probably flourishing in 1597–1598, about the pre-eminence of Court, Country, or City as a mode of life.

Line 8: Remoras (cf. note on *Loves Progress*) were fabled to be able to stop ships.

Line 18: both poisonous creatures, either of which might be its own antidote, but not so in combination.

H: W: IN HIBER: BELLIGERANTI

The title abbreviates "Henrico Wottoni in Hibernia belligeranti" (to Henry Wotton making war in Ireland). Wotton did so in 1599.

TO SIR EDWARD HERBERT, AT JULYERS: ("Man is a lumpe")

Sir Edward Herbert, later Lord Herbert of Cherbury, was at the siege of Juliers in 1610. The son of Lady Magdalen Herbert and the elder brother of George Herbert, he was a poet, philosopher, pioneer Deist, and a somewhat eccentric egotist. The poem addresses him in his role as a philosopher, and is a good example of Donne's imaginative versifying of argument.

Lines 23-24: hemlock nourishes chickens but poisons men.

TO MR. T. W.: ("Hast thee harsh verse")

Written to Thomas Woodward during the London plague. The poem will be Donne's testament if he dies of it. Note that it can be regarded as an irregular sonnet.

ANNIVERSARIES

These, the first published of Donne's poems, were written to celebrate the first and second anniversaries of the death in 1610 of the fifteen-year-old Elizabeth Drury, the daughter of his wealthy patron, Sir Robert Drury. Of their subject Ben Jonson said to Drummond "That Donnes Anniversaries were profane and full of blasphemies: that he told Mr. Done if it had been written of the Virgin Marie it had been something; to which he answered that he described the Idea of a Woman, and not as she was." Donne's own apology for the quite fantastic eulogy has been echoed in various forms by modern critics: Grierson suggests that Dante's canonization of Beatrice was a partial model, Marjorie Nicolson (see Bibliography) has elaborately anatomized the possible identities of the "she" of the poems.

But they are also (and more importantly) solemn meditations on death, in complementary division: the first on the Contempt of the World, the second on the Glories of Paradise. As Louis Martz has demonstrated, they use much of the framework of traditional devotional forms. Yet old forms are transfused by an acute sensitivity to new discovery in geography, astronomy, and physiology, and to the general condition of the poet's contemporary world.

AN ANATOMIE OF THE WORLD: THE FIRST ANNIVERSARY

Lines 205 ff.: *new Philosophy*: a famous passage, whose theme is the collapse of the patterned harmony at the root of both physical and social theories of Elizabethan world order. Copernicus, Tycho, and Galileo have destroyed the world of concentric spheres and elements, with the "Element of fire" at their outermost: the discovery of novae ("New starres," line 260) in 1572 and 1604 has shaken traditional faith in the permanence of created matter. Individualism, seen in the image of the isolated and self-creating Phoenix (line 217), has broken down the hierarchical order of society, patterned on the family: Father and Son, Lord and Man, Prince and Subject, God and His Children (line 215). Lines 251-301 show the breaking of the circle, the traditional image of harmony and perfection; the last metaphor is from geographical discovery of heights of land (Pico on Tenariffe in the Canaries) and depths of ocean which distort the circularity of the Earth itself.

Lines 265-267: the Tropics of Capricorn and Cancer limit the southern and northern declination of the sun.

Line 380: the father is the heaven, the mother the earth.

Lines 389-390: possibly referring to the serpents made by the casting down of Aaron's and the Egyptian magicians' rods.

Line 464: "Give ear, O ye heavens" (Deut. xxxii, 1-42).

OF THE PROGRESSE OF THE SOULE:
THE SECOND ANNIVERSARY

Line 46: "Gods safe-sealing Bowle" is the communion cup.

Line 127: *Mithridate*: a universal antidote compounded of many ingredients.

Lines 193-206: Note that Donne, presumably for the pictorial quality of his image, here reverts to the Old Philosophy; the order of spheres traversed by the soul is almost precisely that of Dante in the *Paradiso*.

Line 242: *th'Electrum*: an alloy, in which were many degrees of gold.

Lines 271-272: the problem which Harvey must then have been attacking (*De motu cordis* appeared in 1628).

Lines 291-292: note Donne's skepticism of empirical method: "sense and Fantasie" are the sense-impressions we must use as bases for induction.

Line 360: prerogatives of royalty; the following lines enumerate them.

Line 442: the presence of God is both the ultimate object of knowledge, and the means of knowing it.

Line 511: *a place*: France, which Donne was visiting with Sir Robert Drury.

DIVINE POEMS

The latest scholarship tends to date many of the poems rather earlier than formerly, notably the bulk of the *Holy Sonnets*. Helen Gardner argues convincingly against Grierson's assumption that the latter were written as a group, and therefore must be later than the date of the death of Donne's wife in 1617. She places the first twelve in 1609, the next four not later than 1611, and only the three Westmoreland sonnets after 1617. With *La Corona* dated in 1607 and the *Litanie* in 1608, the change would place the bulk of Donne's religious poetry during the period of self-examination at Mitcham, and indicate that after his ordination he did indeed nearly give up versing. The poems that can be definitely dated thereafter are composed for unique occasions—notably the sonnet on his wife's death, the hymn in prospect of his voyage to Germany, and the two hymns in dire sickness.

LA CORONA

These are very probably the "Holy Hymns and Sonnets" sent to Mrs. Herbert in July, 1607. "Corona" means wreath as well as crown; the first sonnet plays on all the changes.

The symbolic circle is of course made by the carrying over of the last lines (the last line of 7 is also the first line of 1); but it is also worth noting how ingeniously their syntax is varied.

Annunciation: Lines 13-14: possibly Donne's reply to Marlowe's earthly "Infinite riches in a little room."

Crucifying: Line 3: *weake spirits*: the poor in spirit, whose is the kingdom of heaven (Matt., v, 3).

HOLY SONNETS

The text follows Gardner's order, based on the 1633 edition, rather than Grierson's based on 1635; the Roman numeral at the end of each sonnet represents the number in Grierson's order, which has been followed by most modern editions. Gardner points out that the sonnets ordered as she does provide discernible meditative sequences: a group of six on death and judgment, or the Last Things; another of six on the mystery of the Creator's love for his creatures, and the love man owes to God; and one of four (from 1635) on sin and penitence. Only the three Westmoreland sonnets are "separate ejaculations." The first six progress from preparatory prayer, to mortal sickness, to the moment of death, to the Last Judgment, to alternate damnation and the death of Death at the resurrection of the Just.

"Spit in my face," line 7: *inglorious*: Christ had not then been glorified in the Resurrection; but the sense is also ironic. Line 11: Jacob's counterfeit of Esau in the skins of the goats.

"Father, part of his double interest," line 13: *thy lawes abridgement*: "Thou shalt love the Lord thy God. . . . Thou shalt love thy neighbour as thyself" (Matt., xxiii, 37-9); *thy last command*: "A new commandment I give unto you, that ye love one another" (John, xiii, 34).

"If faithfull soules": the sonnet is based on the scholastic distinction between Angelic Knowledge through direct intuition, and human Knowledge through reasoning from evidence.

"Show me deare Christ": Gardner argues that the sonnet should be taken not as Donne's inability to choose even after his ordination between Roman, Calvinistic, and Anglican, but his lament at the contrast between the apostolic vision of a universal Church, and the actual rent and tattered fabric of Christianity in his day.

A LITANIE

A litany is a liturgical prayer of supplication; Donne follows more closely the order of supplication of the English pre-Reformation Sarum rite than that of the Anglican Prayer Book. The inclusion of the Doctors is specifically Roman. However, the stanzas following the roll call of intercessors make it peculiarly personal. Difficulties in the poem arise from the fact that its wit is theological, and its theology often witty. Consult Gardner's notes for further exegesis.

Line 57: the pillar of cloud by day and of fire by night were interpreted as the obscurity of the Old Testament and the light of the Evangelists.

Lines 64-68: the Prophets harmonized the Mosaic law with that of Christ, Whom they foresaw.

Line 74: *this All*: the Apostles encompassed the whole world in their journeys.

Line 99: *Dioclesian*: the archetypal persecutor of Christians.

Lines 167-171: Christ's "free confession" of His identity in the Garden blinded those sent to arrest Him, so that He might have escaped. There is an allusion to the contemporary problem of whether the persecuted priest might ethically deny his calling.

Lines 240-241: scientific study of Nature is "nothing" without knowledge of its Creator.

Line 252: sin is "nothing" because it is the privation of good.

THE CROSSE

The extreme Puritans attacked even "Materiall Crosses" as idols; Donne is defending their possession, and in so doing he finds patterns of them, as well as the uses of penitence, in (it will seem) everything.

UPON THE ANNUNCIATION AND PASSION FALLING UPON ONE DAY. 1608

In 1608 Good Friday fell on March 25, the annual date of Lady Day. This provides the occasion for the central conceit of the poem, the circle of beginnings and endings.

Line 17: *Orbitie*: bereavement.

Lines 25-30: the Church is like the North Star, by which mariners guide themselves even though it is not the true pole.

GOODFRIDAY, 1613

Lines 1-6: according to Scholastic astronomy, each celestial sphere was in its "naturall forme" governed by an Angelic intelligence, but might also be subject to "forraigne motions."

Lines 11-28: perhaps Donne's most emotional rendering of the great paradoxes of the Incarnation.

Line 20: the earthquake and eclipse at Christ's crucifixion (Matt., xxvii, 51, 45).

TO MR. TILMAN

Edward Tilman took deacon's orders on Dec. 20, 1618.

Line 43: cf. Walton on Donne's preaching: "always preeching to himselfe, like an Angel from a cloud, but in none."

A HYMNE TO CHRIST AT THE AUTHORS LAST GOING INTO GERMANY

Written before Donne's departure for Germany, May 12, 1619, as chaplain to Lord Doncaster's embassy.

HYMNE TO GOD MY GOD, IN MY SICKNESSE

Walton thought the poem written during Donne's last sickness, but Sir Julius Caesar dated it from his earlier grave illness in 1623; there has been much modern controversy. The image of the patient as flat map is also used (much extended) in the fourth Meditation of the *Devotions*, which were certainly a product of the earlier illness.

Line 9: *South-west discoverie*: Donne's witty turn on the much-sought Northwest Passage; south is the symbolic region of heat or fever, west of death.

Line 10: *per fretum febris*: through the raging straits of fever; *fretum* means both "raging" and "strait."

Line 16: "home" is Paradise; there were various speculations as to its terrestrial location.

Line 18: *Anyan*: Bering Strait.

Line 20: Europe, the inheritance of Noah's son Japhet; Africa, of Ham; and Asia, of Shem.

Line 30: Donne is probably turning to his occasion Psalm cxlv, 14: "The Lord upholdeth all that fall, and raiseth up all those that be bowed down."

A HYMNE TO GOD THE FATHER

According to Walton, written during the illness of 1623. The poem of course turns on the pun done-Donne; there is a further pun on sun-Son in line 15.